Today's
ROYAL AIR FORCE
in Colour

A Tornado F.2 from No 229 OCU is shown here in formation with one of the BBMF's Spitfires with which it flies at a number of airshows, displaying its low speed capabilities.

Today's
ROYAL AIR FORCE
in Colour

Jeremy Flack

BLANDFORD PRESS
POOLE · NEW YORK · SYDNEY

First published in the UK 1987 by Blandford Press
Link House, West Street, Poole, Dorset BH15 1LL

Copyright © 1987 Jeremy Flack/Aviation
Photographs International – Swindon

Distributed in the United States by
Sterling Publishing Co, Inc,
2 Park Avenue, New York, NY 10016

Distributed in Australia by
Capricorn Link (Australia) Pty Ltd
PO Box 665, Lane Cove, NSW 2066

British Library Cataloguing in Publication Data
Flack, Jeremy
    Today's Royal Air Force in colour.
    1. Great Britain. *Royal Air Force*
    I. Title
    358.4′00941   UG635.G7

ISBN 0 7137 1644 4 (hardback)

Editor: M. G. Burns

Typeset by Keyspools Ltd, Golborne, Lancs
Printed in Great Britain by Purnell Book Production Ltd.
Member of the BPCC Group

FOR JULIE, LUCY AND LORETTA

Contents

Introduction	7
RAF Strike Command	11
No 1 Group	13
Hercules	33
Air-to-Air Refuelling	46
No 11 Group	51
No 18 Group	71
Nimrod	74
Search & Rescue	80
Overseas Bases	86
RAF Germany	88
RAF Support Command	100
Central Flying School	108
Air Cadets	112
RAF Regiment	123
Index	127

A busy line of Harrier GR.3s and T.4s of No. 233 OCU at RAF Wittering.

Introduction

Since the Royal Air Force was formed in 1918, it has seen a never ending series of changes whilst struggling to keep up to date with the ever-advancing performances, and never more so than today. With hardware costing astronomic sums of money and technology leaping forward at an increasing rate, it becomes progressively more difficult to keep the equipment current and prevent it becoming obsolete. The RAF is going through a major updating of its aircraft stocks and has to be extremely careful with its selection since they will be in service for many years to come.

Aircraft that have given faithful service since the fifties have nearly all been retired. The Vulcan, which was in the process of being scrapped, was given a stay of execution and saw action during the

Tornado F.2
The Tornado is rapidly becoming the backbone of the RAF, providing both strike and air defence capabilities, and will be operated well into the next century. A total of 394 Tornados has been ordered for the RAF, of which eighteen are the F.2 variant (illustrated) and 147 F.3s for air defence (IDS). In addition, 112 IDS have been ordered for the West German Navy, 212 for their air force plus 35 ECM variants, 100 IDS for the Italian Air Force, 48 IDS plus 24 ADV for the Saudi Air Force and eight ADV for the Omani Air Force.

Tucano T.1
The Tucano T.1 is the Shorts-built version of the Brazilian Embraer EMB-312. It is powered by the Garrett TPE-12B. This advanced basic trainer, of which 130 have been ordered for the RAF, will replace the Jet Provost.

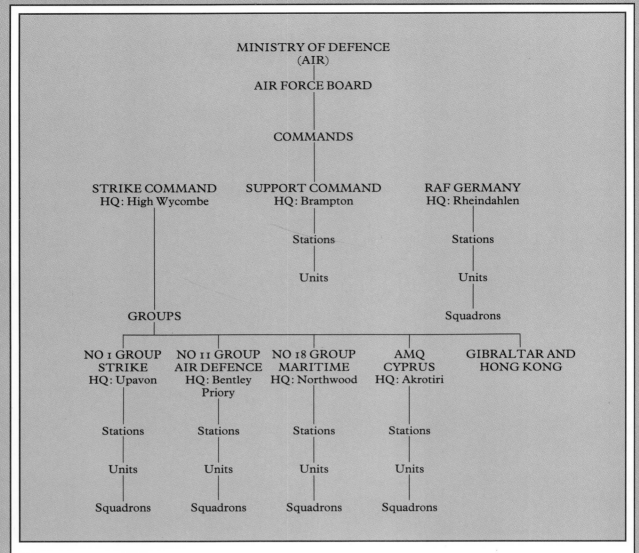

MINISTRY OF DEFENCE
(AIR)

AIR FORCE BOARD

COMMANDS

STRIKE COMMAND	SUPPORT COMMAND	RAF GERMANY
HQ: High Wycombe	HQ: Brampton	HQ: Rheindahlen
	Stations	Stations
	Units	Units
GROUPS		Squadrons

NO 1 GROUP STRIKE	NO 11 GROUP AIR DEFENCE	NO 18 GROUP MARITIME	AMQ CYPRUS	GIBRALTAR AND HONG KONG
HQ: Upavon	HQ: Bentley Priory	HQ: Northwood	HQ: Akrotiri	
Stations	Stations	Stations	Stations	
Units	Units	Units	Units	
Squadrons	Squadrons	Squadrons	Squadrons	

Falklands campaign but has now become a museum object. The Whirlwind helicopter, a familiar sight around the British coastline, has now been replaced by the Wessex and Sea King. The Devon communications aircraft has now been superseded by the HS.125. Once the mainstay of the RAF's fighter and ground attack forces, the Hunter has now only a token presence. The Shackleton, whose ancestry descends from the Lincoln and is the RAF's last remaining front-line piston-engined aircraft, is awaiting the belated arrival of the new AEW aircraft. The Canberra bomber, which, like the Hunter, was once part of the backbone of the RAF, now only serves lesser duties in small numbers.

The new backbone for the RAF of today and tomorrow is the Tornado. Being delivered in two forms, it has or will replace a number of previous types. In the strike-attack-reconnaissance roles the Tornado GR.1 has replaced the Vulcan and Canberra and has partially replaced the Buccaneer and Jaguar. In the interceptor role, the Tornado F.2 and F.3 will be replacing the Lightning and Phantom. Subject to much embarrassment and discussion is the continued delay of the Nimrod AEW's entry into operational service, which has resulted in the retention in service of the Shackleton long after it was due for retirement.

The Victor tanker fleet soldiers on in one remaining squadron but its days are now limited, especially after the number of hours that were flown in support of and as part of Operation

Harrier GR.5

The Harrier GR.5 is the latest addition to the unique V/STOL aircraft family. This re-designed Harrier, powered by the Rolls-Royce Pegasus 105 vectored thrust engine, has a greater range plus warload capability together with updated electronics. It will become an even more impressive aircraft than the Harrier GR.3s and Sea Harriers which were so successful during the Falklands conflict. A total of 62 has been ordered for the RAF plus 328 of the US version, designated AV-8B, ordered for the US Marine Corps and twelve for the Spanish Navy. The AV-8B batches include some two-seat trainers. The RAF has ordered long-lead items for a further 27 GR.5s.

CORPORATE in the South Atlantic in 1982. The Victors have been augmented by the conversion of five Standard and four Super VC.10s bought from surplus airline stocks which are now in service in the tanker role. Further ex-airline VC.10s have been purchased and it is possible that more may be converted. In addition, six Tristars are being converted for a dual role of transport and tanker.

The long-missed heavy-lift helicopter capability has been filled by the Chinook and, although a number were lost during the sinking of the *Atlantic Conveyor* during the Falklands campaign, these have more than been replaced by the re-ordering of seven more examples. To replace the UK Air Defence Phantoms of No 23 Squadron which are now based in the Falklands, twelve ex-

US Navy Phantom F-4Js have been purchased and are in service with No 74 Squadron. The delivery of the 62 Harrier GR.5s on order is now much awaited, as is the controversial order from Shorts for the Tucano which will replace the Jet Provosts.

It was planned that the RAF would enter a new era when Squadron Leader Nigel Wood became the first Briton in Space in June 1986. He was to have joined a Shuttle crew for the launch of the Skynet 4a satellites. However, following the tragic Shuttle disaster this has been temporarily halted.

The 1980s have seen the re-introduction of the Royal Auxiliary Air Force Squadrons to assist the RAF in a number of functions.

ACKNOWLEDGEMENTS

I would like to thank the following for their very much appreciated help and assistance: Sqn Ldr Anderson; Keith Ansell; Jeremy Baldwin; Robin Barrett; Sqn Ldr Bingham; Maj Birchwood; David Bland; Sqn Ldr Cooper; Flt Lt Cross; Sqn Ldr Day; Dave Dickinson; Barry Ellson; Tony Fenn; Hugh Field; Julie Flack; Loretta Flack; Lucy Flack; Sqn Ldr Glenn; John Godden; Sqn Ldr Haggett; Sqn Ldr Harrison; Flt Lt Hartill; David Healey; Terry Heffernan; Sqn Ldr Hughes; David Kamiya; Brian Lawrence; Tim Lewis; Sqn Ldr McLain; Flt Lt Miles; Sqn Ldr Neil; Sqn Ldr Newman; Flt Lt Ogg; Sqn Ldr Patterson; Wing Cdr Peacock-Edwards; Michael Pentrith; Air Com Probert; Simon Raynes; Flt Lt Read; Air Com Robson; MALM Rodmell; David Rose; Wg Cdr Roser; Chris Shepherd; Sqn Ldr Sporr; Flt Lt Stonham; Flt Lt Strachan; Flt Lt Stuart; Flt Lt Tarrant; Wg Cdr Taylor; Flt Lt Thorn; Sqn Ldr Timms; Flt Lt Toogood; Flt Lt Tredry; Alan Waddington; Wg Cdr Williams; Flt Lt Williams; and Flt Lt Yetman.

I would also like to thank the numerous members of the Royal Air Force, Fleet Air Arm, Army, United States Air Force, International Air Tattoo and Society of British Aerospace Companies for their valued assistance.

All photographs in this book are by the author except the following: British Aerospace Front cover, 9, 27 top, 41 top, 47 top, 70, 108; Shorts 7; RAF 16, 38; Brian Lawrence 28, 94, 109, back cover; Steve Howard 67; Tony Rodmell 86; Barry Ellson/RAFG 93.

RAF Strike Command

Strike Command came into being with the merger of the main teeth of the Royal Air Force—Bomber and Fighter Commands. They were later joined by Coastal Command which became No 18 (Maritime) Group and Signals Command which became No 90 (Signal) Group but was later transferred back to Support Command. On 1 September 1972, Air Support Command was also absorbed.

In 1975, the integration of Strike Command within NATO was made when the Air Officer Commanding-in-Chief was appointed a major subordinate commander under the Supreme Allied Commander Europe (SACEUR) with the NATO title of Commander-in-Chief United Kingdom Air Forces (CINCUKAIR).

Strike Command is based at RAF High Wycombe and comprises three Groups. No 1 Group is responsible for the nuclear strike, conventional attack, reconnaissance, air-to-air refuelling and transport. No 11 Group for air defence, and No 18 Group for long-range maritime reconnaissance and rescue.

One of Strike Command's main responsibilities is for the United Kingdom Air Defence Region (UKADR) within which No 11 Group's Phantom and Lightning fighters regularly intercept long range Soviet aircraft. These interceptions are frequently made by the Lightnings and Phantoms that are kept on Quick Reaction Alert (QRA) and scrambled when a possible intruder is tracked on

No 111 Squadron

A successful APC at RAF Akrotiri is celebrated by members of No 111 Squadron from RAF Leuchars. The banner draped across the Phantom is one of the targets which are towed behind Canberras from No 100 Squadron. The marks on the banner are hits by the 20 mm shells which have paint on their tips leaving stain around the holes enabling the weapons instructors to identify which of the crews have scored the hits.

radar. This may be by ground radar in the UK but is more likely to be by another NATO nation's radars or by one of the Shackleton AEW.2s from RAF Lossiemouth. The fighters are vectored by ground controllers until they have contact on their own radar or have a visual. If the aircraft is an intruding Soviet aircraft it is escorted away from British airspace. The fighters are kept airborne by Victor and VC.10 tanker aircraft keeping their fuel tanks topped up during flight.

Over the next few years, the Lightnings and Phantoms will be replaced by the Tornado F.3 which has better radar capabilities and endurance. It is hoped that the Shackletons will be replaced by the Nimrod AEW.3 but delays in the programme are making this seem to be unlikely while the Boeing E-3A Sentry becomes a strong contender. The Victor and VC.10 tankers are being augmented by Tristar tankers. In time of tension or conflict, the Hawks from the Tactical Weapons Units would be fitted with Sidewinder air-to-air missiles and used as a second line of defence, operating between the main fighter force out over the North Sea and the UK coastline. Any intruder getting past these aircraft would be attacked from the ground by surface-to-air missiles (SAM) Bloodhounds and Rapiers.

All front line airfields are subjected to Tactical Evaluations (TACEVAL) which are exercises to test the station's ability to come to a war footing and carry out its role at very short notice. This may take the form of a series of surprise attacks by a simulated enemy during which aircraft may be destroyed, runways damaged and key officers killed. The attacks may also simulate the use of chemical or biological weapons in which case NCB clothing must be worn. It is then the job of the rest of the station to maintain their task. At the end of the TACEVAL the station and its squadrons will be assessed as to their level of preparation for conflict. Any shortcomings can then be corrected.

In addition to the airfields in the UK, Strike Command is responsible for all of the overseas bases with the exception of those in Germany. These include RAF Akrotiri in Cyprus where No 84 Squadron flies in support of UNFICYP as well as providing SAR for visiting RAF aircraft during their Armament Practice Camps. Each RAF fighter squadron visits RAF Akrotiri once a year for live gunnery experience, firing at a target banner towed by a Canberra from No 100 Squadron. In addition, an RAF Regiment Field Squadron is based at RAF Akrotiri for airfield defence although this would be transferred to Germany in time of tension.

Since the Falklands conflict, RAF Stanley and subsequently RAF Mount Pleasant have required a substantial force to be maintained on permanent readiness. No 23 Squadron, equipped with the Phantom FGR.2, has been based in the South Atlantic since the reopening of RAF Stanley. No 1453 Flight, with Harrier GR.3s, was based at RAF Stanley until the opening of RAF Mount Pleasant in 1985. SAR cover is provided by the Sea King HAR.3s of No 78 Squadron, the tanker capacity by Hercules C.1Ks of No 1312 Flight and heavy lift helicopter operations by No 78 Squadron Chinooks.

No 28 Squadron at RAF Sek Kong in Hong Kong assists in the defence and policing of British interests in the protectorate. In addition, Strike Command administers RAF Gibraltar and detachments at Offutt Air Force Base in Nebraska, USA, and Goose Bay in Labrador, Canada, to support overseas training exercises.

No 1 Group

No 1 Group is responsible for the control and training of the RAF's UK-based strike and attack aircraft, tactical reconnaissance, tankers, strategic and tactical transport plus air and helicopter support for the Army.

During the 1980s, No 1 Group has been undergoing a major transformation with the Vulcan fleet retired and the numbers of Buccaneers, Canberras and Victors reduced. These aircraft have been replaced by the Panavia Tornado GR.1 in the strike and attack roles. Tornados will eventually replace the last remaining Canberra PR.9s as well as the Jaguar GR.1s of No 41 Squadron in the reconnaissance role.

The Victor K.2 tankers are gradually being withdrawn with the completion of the deliveries to No 101 Squadron of the VC10 K.2 and K.3 and when the last of the Tristars are received by No 214 Squadron, the last remaining Victor unit, No 55 Squadron, will be disbanded. By the time that these changes to the tanker fleet have been completed, it will have doubled its fuel off-loading capacity.

The VC.10 C.1 will remain the backbone of No 1 Group's Strategic transport, together with the Tristar K.1 and KC.1 tankers will retain a transport role. The Hercules is No 1 Group's tactical transport workhorse and modifications to 30 of the 66 delivered has enabled even greater flexibility.

The number of Harriers at RAF Wittering will soon be increased with the introduction of the GR.5 which, together with the Jaguars, provide offensive support for the army. The Pumas and Wessex provide logistical helicopter support which has been greatly increased with the introduction of the heavy-lift Chinook. These aircraft are assigned to NATO's ACE Mobile Force (AMF). As such, they would be rushed straight to any area of tension along with units from other member countries to show the aggressor that NATO's resolve of an attack against one member will be considered an attack against all.

No 1 Group also administers The Queen's Flight, which is in the process of replacing its Andover CC.2s with the BAe 146, and No 32 Squadron, used for VIP transport. In addition, No 1 Group has responsibility for the Andover E.3s of No 115 Squadron, used for calibration duties, and some squadrons of the RAF Regiment.

No 1 Group, Strike Command—High Wycombe

No 1 Sqn	Harrier GR.3, T.4	Wittering
No 6 Sqn	Jaguar GR.1, T.2	Coltishall
No 7 Sqn	Chinook HC.1	Odiham
No 10 Sqn	VC-10 C.1	Brize Norton
No 24 Sqn	Hercules from LTW	Lyneham
No 27 Sqn	Tornado GR.1	Marham
No 30 Sqn	Hercules from LTW	Lyneham
No 32 Sqn	Andover CC.2; HS.125 CC.1, CC.2, CC.3; Gazelle HCC.4	Northolt
No 33 Sqn	Puma HC.1	Odiham
No 41 Sqn	Jaguar GR.1, T.2	Coltishall
No 45 Sqn (Shadow Sqn for TWCU)	Tornado GR.1	Honington
No 47 Sqn	Hercules from LTW	Lyneham
No 54 Sqn	Jaguar GR.1, T.2	Coltishall
No 55 Sqn	Victor K.2	Marham
No 70 Sqn	Hercules from LTW	Lyneham
No 72 Sqn	Wessex HC.2	Aldergrove
No 78 Sqn	Chinook HC.1; Sea King HAR.3	Mount Pleasant
No 101 Sqn	VC-10; Victor K.2, K.3	Brize Norton
No 115 Sqn	Andover E.3	Benson

No 216 Sqn	Tristar K.1, KC.1, K.2	Brize Norton
No 617 Sqn	Tornado GR.1	Marham
No 226 OCU	Jaguar GR.1, T.2	Lossiemouth
No 233 OCU	Harrier GR.3, T.4	Wittering
No 240 OCU	Puma HC.1; Chinook HC.1	Odiham
No 241 OCU	VC-10 C.1 borrowed from No 10 Sqn	Brize Norton
No 242 OCU	Hercules from LTW	Lyneham
Andover Training Flight	Andover E.3 borrowed from No 115 Sqn	Benson
The Queen's Flight	Andover CC.2; Wessex HCC.4; BAe 146 CC.2	Benson
No 1312 Flight	Hercules C.1K	Mount Pleasant
No 1417 Flight	Harrier GR.3	Belize
No 1563 Flight	Puma HC.1	Belize
Tri-National Tornado Training Establishment	Tornado GR.1, GR(T).1	Cottesmore
Tornado Weapons Conversion Unit	Tornado GR.1 (No 45 Sqn—Shadow Sqn)	Honington
Lyneham Tactical Wing	Hercules C.1, C.1P, C.1K, C.3	Lyneham
Fire Fighting School	—	Manston

RAF Regiment

No 2 Sqn	Light Armour	Hullavington
No 15 Sqn	Light Armour	Hullavington
No 51 Sqn	Light Armour	Catterick
No 58 Sqn	Light Armour	Catterick

Royal Auxiliary Air Force

No 4624 Sqn	Movements	Brize Norton
No 4626 Sqn	Aeromedical/Medivac	Wroughton

No 1 Squadron

No 1 Squadron was the world's first operational VTOL unit. The Harrier GR.3 is capable of flying from rough unprepared sites. It can carry a wide selection of weaponry on its five hard points depending on the mission. Its roles include ground attack, air defence and, fitted with a F95 oblique camera, reconnaissance. The Falklands conflict tested the Harriers and their crew to the full. Although their normal radius of action is 400 miles, they were flown 8,000 miles from the UK to the South Atlantic with one intermediate stop at Ascension with assistance from in-flight refuelling. The longest leg took 9 hours 15 minutes. During the eleven-week war the ten RAF Harriers flew nearly 150 missions against ground targets.

No 1453 Flight

At the end of the Falklands conflict, the RAF Harriers in the South Atlantic were formed into No 1453 Flight and were retained at RAF Stanley for air defence, supported by the Royal Navy Sea Harriers. The Sea Harriers gave way to RAF Phantoms once the runway was lengthened, but No 1453 Flight remained and was normally seen armed with Sidewinder missiles. The Flight was disbanded in 1985 with the opening of RAF Mount Pleasant. The elongated nose contains the Ferranti Laser Ranging and Marked Target Seeker (LRMTS) to improve the close support capability over the battlefield. It proved to be highly effective during the conflict.

No 1417 Flight

In 1975, a detachment of Harriers were deployed to Belize in response to a build up of Guatemalan troops along her borders. A signal to Guatemala that any action against its neighbour would be considered a threat to British interests, the deployment of No 1417 Flight with Harrier GR.3s was a gesture of the British Government's resolve. Should they be required, re-inforcements could be flown out from the UK in a matter of a few hours with the help of air-to-air refuelling.

A total of 114 Harrier GR.1/3s was ordered for the RAF, together with 12 T.2/4s. The type also serves with the Royal Navy, US Marine Corps, Indian Navy, and the Spanish Navy. The two-seat T.4 trainers are fitted with the same operational equipment as the single seat GR.3s and can carry the same weapons on the same missions. The fuselage of the RAF Harriers has 90 per cent commonality with that of the RN Sea Harriers but only 10 per cent of the avionics are common to both.

No 233 OCU
A Harrier GR.3 of No 233 OCU based at RAF Wittering takes off from a grass strip. Its peacetime function is to train aircrew ready for their posting to No 1 Squadron which is also at RAF Wittering or either Nos 3 or 4 Squadrons in RAF Germany, but it would become fully operational in time of conflict.

No 6 Squadron *Opposite top*
Based at RAF Coltishall, No 6 Squadron is one of two equipped with the Jaguar GR.1s for the attack/strike role. A product of Anglo-French collaboration, the Jaguar is designed to fly at low level with a selection from an impressive array of weapons fitted to the four underwing hard points. Together with No 54 Squadron, No 6 Squadron is assigned to the SACEUR Strategic Reserve (Air) and could be called upon to deploy at short notice to any airfield in mainland Europe. Thus, Nos 6 and 54 Squadrons regularly fly to various airfields, at the same time practising air-to-air refuelling. The three Jaguar GR.1s are shown here taking off with the aid of reheat from RAF Akrotiri after training for such a deployment.

No 54 Squadron *Opposite*
The other Jaguar GR.1 attack/strike unit based at RAF Coltishall is No 54 Squadron. It is fitted with two weapon delivery systems. One is the extremely accurate Laser Ranging and Marked Target Seeker, used in conjunction with a ground-based laser target designator. The other system is a highly advanced automated navigation and attack system complete with a moving map display and a head-up display (HUD). On its pylons, the Jaguar is able to carry up to eight free fall or retarded 1,000 lb bombs. It can also carry the BL755 cluster bomb, which is highly effective in the interdiction role. It can also carry nuclear weapons. It is shown here fitted with extra fuel tanks on the inboard pylons and practice bombs on the outer pylons.

No 226 OCU

RAF Lossiemouth houses No 226 OCU, the Jaguar Operational Conversion Unit. In 1973, it became the first recipient of the 165 Jaguar GR.1s and 38 T.2s built for the RAF. At the OCU, crews are taught low-level flying, to enable them to keep below the radar horizon. Its small size and lack of tell-tale smoke trail makes the Jaguar a difficult target to spot at altitudes below 250 ft.

The Jaguar is supersonic at all altitudes, and can operate from semi-prepared or grass runways. It has a range of up to 2,000 miles and a maximum weapon load of 10,500 lb.

No 7 Squadron

The introduction of the Boeing Vertol Chinook into service with No 7 Squadron at RAF Odiham saw the revival of the RAF's heavy lift helicopter capability which had been lacking since the withdrawal of the Belvedere. Capable of flying with a payload of 20,000 lb, the Chinook has a range of 250 miles and a speed of 175 knots. The Chinook has three under fuselage lifting points as well as a large rear ramp door which permits even a Land Rover to be carried internally. It can carry 44 fully-equipped troops and can be used as an ambulance.

No 78 Squadron

Four Chinook HC.1s were sent to the South Atlantic aboard the ill-fated *Atlantic Conveyor* and three were destroyed when the vessel was hit by an Argentinian Exocet. The survivor was operated out of Port San Carlos, kept operational, having lost its support equipment on the *Atlantic Conveyor*, through the skill of its resourceful support detachment. In the 150 hours flown, the single Chinook carried 1530 troops and 600 tons of equipment in addition to 650 prisoners of war. On one flight, in response to an operational emergency, 81 troops were carried—nearly twice the normal limit. Initially numbered No 1310 Flight, and located near San Carlos at Kelley's Garden, it was amalgamated with No 1564 Flight (Sea Kings) to become No 78 Squadron and is based at RAF Mount Pleasant.

No 240 OCU

No 240 OCU operates both the Chinook HC.1 and the Puma HC.1 to train pilots that have been streamed at No 2 Flying Training School, and also trains navigators and crewmen. The Chinook pilots fly approximately 45 hours while at the OCU. After completing their course, they join their operational squadron as co-pilots. The Chinook crews also practise flying procedures on the British Airways simulator.

No 9 Squadron

The Tornado is the result of a Tri-national development effort designed to meet the military threat to Europe. It demonstrates NATO's resolve to standardise equipment wherever possible within the Alliance. Designed to raise the nuclear threshold, the highly flexible Tornado reduces NATO's need to resort to nuclear weapons. No 9 Squadron became the first squadron to fly the Tornado GR.1. One of their Tornados is seen (*above*) with the Vulcan B.2 with which it was previously equipped. On 1 October, No 9 Squadron moved to RAF Bruggen, joining RAFG. *Right*: The Tornado can carry in excess of 16,000 lb of weapons on external pylons, three under the fuse-lage and four underwing and deliver them accurately on target in all weathers. This GR.1 of No 9 Squadron is fitted with Sky Shadow ECM pods on the outer wings, fuel tanks on the wing pylons and 1,000 lb bombs.

No 27 Squadron

The Tornado GR.1 is able to carry existing and future weapons at very low level together with ECM equipment to reduce its vulnerability. With minimum distance take-off and landing runs, it can operate off short lengths of concrete, such as taxi ways, should the runway be knocked out. It also has reduced dependence on ground supply equipment. This Tornado GR.1 is from No 27 Squadron, based at RAF Marham and uses reheat for take-off.

No 45 Squadron

No 45 Squadron is the 'shadow' squadron for the Tactical Weapons Conversion Unit (TWCU) based at RAF Honington. Equipped with the Tornado GR.1, the TWCU is used to complete the training of aircrews before they join operational squadrons in roles ranging from battlefield interdiction and counter strike to reconnaissance. The Tornado GR.1 is powered by two Turbo-Union RB 199–34 engines, a short and light unit which has a thrust-weight ratio of over eight to one. It uses advanced technology to obtain low specific fuel consumption which is essential for high speed low-level flight with a high weapons load and good range.

No 9 Squadron *Opposite top*

Two Tornado GR Mk 1s of No 9 Squadron from RAF Honington, each carrying four 1,000 lb bombs, two full wing tanks and two ECM pods, practise very low-level flying using their terrain following capability. The Tornado is an outstanding aircraft, designed to fly transonic speeds at very low altitude, hugging the ground using automatic terrain following and able to hit the target by day or night.

No 617 Squadron *Opposite below*

A Tornado GR.1 of No 617 Squadron, based at RAF Marham, stands outside an HAS. On completion of trials, it is planned to fit the BAe Linescan 4000 to the Tornado GR.1 which will give it a reconnaissance system in advance of any other. Using infra-red and video it will enable the crew to detect heat sources by day or night and in any weather. They would therefore be able to detect buildings, vehicles, equipment and personnel, even when hidden by camouflage nets. The navigator will be able to monitor any identified targets on a TV screen, and will be able to magnify at the touch of a button any detail shown on the screen which remains constant despite the high speed manoeuvring of the aircraft.

TTTE

The Tri-National Tornado Training Establishment (TTTE) was formed in January 1981 at RAF Cottesmore. It is the first multi-national aircraft programme to contain standardisation through to operational training on the conversion course. At its peak, the TTTE will train 150 crew during a 15-course year, flying 50 aircraft drawn from each of the British, German and Italian Air Forces, as illustrated here, plus the German Navy. This number will drop once all the operational squadrons have formed.

During the four-month course the pilot and navigator will stay together and remain as a crew while flying Tornados. The course will include formation, terrain following and tactical training, including simulated ground attack.

TWCU

The RAF Tornado crews join the Tactical Weapons Conversion Unit (TWCU) based at RAF Honington on completion of their course at the TTTE. Although the TTTE is a multi-national unit, the TWCU is purely RAF, the German and Italian crews having their own versions. This aircraft was photographed before the designation of No 45 Squadron as the shadow squadron.

This TWCU Tornado GR.1 displays a selection of weapons systems. A new weapon has joined the inventory of the RAF, the JP233 area denial weapon, developed and being built by Huntings. Designed for several purposes, a typical role could be to drop a combination of concrete penetration plus anti-personnel warheads on an airfield to knock out the runway and leave the area mined to delay any repairs being made.

No 229 OCU

No 229 OCU received the first of the complement of Tornado F.2s at the end of 1984 and by the middle of 1985 was training the first of the Air Defence crews. During 1986, deliveries commenced of the Tornado F.3 which has updated avionics including the automatic wing sweep, more powerful RB.199 Mk 104 engines and a slightly longer fuselage to assist supersonic stability. In the meantime, the F.2s are being placed in storage as deliveries of the F.3 progress. Once all squadrons have re-equipped, the OCU's F.2s will be returned to them from storage, up-dated to approximately F.3 standard but designated F.2A.

The Tornado F.2 was designed to meet the MoD Air Staff Target 395 for a fighter interceptor for the UK Air Defence Region together with Fleet Protection. It is 80 per cent common with the GR.1. The most visual difference is the 4.5-ft longer nose for the GEC Foxhunter radar and an additional 200 Imperial gallons of fuel. The Foxhunter radar is capable of detecting multiple targets up to 100 miles away. This, together with the Tornado F.2's ability to patrol for several hours 300–400 miles from base and at speeds ranging from 800 knots at sea level to Mach 2.2 at altitude, will greatly increase the effectiveness of No 11 Group. This patrol time would be extended through air-to-air refuelling. The internal avionics fit is very different to the Tornado GR.1's, with an inertial navigation system, air data computer and threat warning receiver. The F.2 would normally operate in close contact with ground defence control via a secure data link together with Nimrod AEW.3s and tankers.

No 10 Squadron

The Vickers VC.10 C.1 has been the last of the strategic transport aircraft until the introduction of the Tristar. Fourteen aircraft were delivered to No 10 Squadron at RAF Brize Norton in the mid 1960s, but following modification by Rolls Royce one has since been scrapped since it was uneconomic to return to standard on completion of RB.211 engine trials. The VC.10 regularly flies throughout the world carrying up to 150 troops or 54,000 lb of freight or any combination of both. The VC.10 weighs some 144 tons and is capable of 560 mph. A fully loaded VC.10 can fly 3,700 miles although this can be extended to 4,900 miles with 29,500 lb payload. The VC.10 C.1 has been built to make use of in-flight refuelling, but this is not currently used.

Right: A typical VC.10 C.1 medivac layout as used in the medical centre for training purposes.

No 241 OCU

No 241 OCU, also based at RAF Brize Norton, is responsible for training crews for the VC.10s and Tristars. It has no aircraft of its own but borrows aircraft from the squad- rons as required. No 241 OCU has also assisted in a two year RAF evalu- ation of a pair of BAe 146 transport aircraft. As a result, two aircraft joined The Queen's Flight in 1986.

Hercules

All RAF Hercules are operated by the Lyneham Tactical Wing (LTW) on a pool basis, except those of No 1312 Flight. The LTW comprises Nos 24, 30, 47 and 70 Squadrons plus No 242 OCU.

A total of 66 Hercules were ordered for the RAF. Built by Lockheed, the RAF's Hercules is similar to the C-130E but is powered by four of the more powerful 4,910 eshp Allison turboprop engines and equipped with British avionics. They were designated C-130K by Lockheed. It is capable of carrying 20,000 lb for 4,600 miles, but the payload can be increased to 45,000 lb, when the range drops to 2,500 miles. The Hercules is capable of carrying a wide range of loads. These can include 92 troops, 62 paratroops, 74 stretchers, two Scout helicopters or 30,000 lb platforms on a roller floor for para-drops. The problem the RAF found when flying the Hercules in support of the Army was that the aircraft 'bulked out' before it was near to its maximum payload. As a result, the RAF ordered 30 Hercules C.1 to be converted to C.3 by Marshalls of Cambridge. This involved the lengthening of the fuselage by the insertion of an 8 ft 4 in plug forward of the wing and 6 ft 8 in aft. This extension increased the volume of the hold from 127.4 to 171.5 cubic metres, typically increasing the load from three Land Rovers and two trailers to four Land Rovers and three trailers. Most of the Army support flying is carried out by Nos 47 and 70 Squadrons.

No 1312 Flight

No 1312 Flight is based at RAF Stanley in the Falkland Islands. It is equipped with Hercules C.1K and flies in support of the Phantoms from No 23 Squadron. The return to the UK of the Harriers and the opening of RAF Mount Pleasant with its longer runway allowing higher Phantom take-off weights, should reduce the strain on this small unit.

Nos 24 and 30 Squadrons are used mainly in the route flying role. The Falklands conflict produced the biggest strain on the transport fleet since the Berlin airlift. Assisted by VC.10s, 707s and Belfasts, some 15,000 hours were flown, during which 7,000 tons of freight was carried, plus 114 vehicles, 22 helicopters and nearly 6,000 troops and support personnel. In an extraordinarily short time, sixteen Hercules were modified, tested and approved for air-to-air refuelling which allowed them to fly to the South Atlantic and air drop vital payloads to the Task Force. On cessation of hostilities, the Hercules C.1P continued to operate a regular flight schedule while the runway at RAF Stanley was being rebuilt. In a matter of weeks, the crews of RAF Hercules were doubling the endurance of the aircraft as a matter of routine. On one such mission, Flt Lt Locke and his crew from No 70 Squadron had the misfortune to hit a headwind in both directions. The flight lasted 28 hours and 3 minutes, longer than any of Lockheed's previous endurance records.

Another modification made to six Hercules was to convert them to tankers for air-to-air refuelling to reduce the strain that was being placed on the tanker fleet. Although too late to take part in Operation CORPORATE, the Hercules have since been used on the air bridge and in the Falklands.

In addition to their normal roles, the RAF Hercules have been involved in a number of humanitarian airlifts. The most well-known has been called Operation BUSHELL by the RAF. It involved a long detachment of two Hercules to Ethiopia to fly in emergency food supplies to famine zones. Averaging ten hours' flying a day, the RAF Hercules had carried 70 per cent of all loads in their first six months. The operation finished at the end of 1985.

LTW *Above and right*
In the view above, one of the two Hercules C.1 detached to Ethiopia to assist in the famine relief is seen staging through Akrotiri, and, right, in flight with the rear ramp lowered, allowing supplies to be air-dropped at low altitude, so allowing greater flexibility in reaching famine areas.

LTW *Left*
A Hercules C.1P in the foreground and a Hercules C.1K operated by Nos 24 and 30 Squadrons plus a VC.10 C.1 from No 10 Squadron on Ascension as part of the air bridge to the Falklands.

No 242 OCU
The Hercules C.1 is capable of air dropping pallets weighing up to 30,000 lb. One technique used for dropping heavy loads is to use a parachute to pull out the pallet whilst flying at very low level, the parachute then acts as a brake.

No 33 Squadron
The Puma HC.1s of No 33 Squadron, based at RAF Odiham, are capable of carrying sixteen troops or 5,500 lb as an underslung load. While out in the field in support of the Army, its high cruising speed of 165 mph enables it quickly to provide logistic support, troop mobility and casualty evacuation and can even be used as a gun-ship when fitted with a GPMG. The No 7 Squadron Chinook in the background would be used for heavy lift support.

No 240 OCU

No 240 OCU trains both Puma HC.1 and Chinook HC.1 pilots who have been streamed at No 2 Flying Training School, plus navigators and crewmen. The Puma crews fly 55 hours and become captains on their completion.

No 1563 Flight

In 1975 three Puma HC.1s were sent to Belize to join No 1417 Flight Harriers to help support the threatened, tiny Central American country. There, they were numbered No 1563 Flight. In 1985, two Pumas were flown to Mexico City to help in the relief operation following the multiple earthquake disaster.

No 72 Squadron

No 72 Squadron has been associated with the Wessex HC.2 since it entered service in 1963. It is now based at RAF Aldergrove in Northern Ireland where it flies in support of the security forces. Developed from the Sikorsky S.58 the Westland Wessex is now rather old but its ability to carry sixteen troops or seven stretchers or up to 3,600 lb as an underslung load still makes it a useful helicopter.

No 115 Squadron

The Hawker Siddeley Andover E.3 is a modification of the C.1 transport aircraft produced especially for ground radio and ground radar calibration duties. Equipped with six aircraft, No 115 Squadron, from its base at RAF Benson, visits each RAF airfield in turn to ensure that all of their radios and radar and navigational systems are extremely accurate. As the aircraft are not in a tactical role, they are painted in a high visibility scheme.

No 32 Squadron

No 32 Squadron, based at RAF Northolt, operates a diverse range of aircraft. It is the RAF's main communications squadron, flying senior Service officers, Government ministers and officials who require to travel by air. The Westland Gazelle HCC.4 has now replaced the Whirl- wind for the shorter flights and the Hawker Siddeley HS.125 is used for the longer distances. The Andover CC.2 is similar to the Hawker Siddeley HS748 short range airliner and can be used when a number of VIPs require to fly to the same destination. A single Andover C.1 was given a plush interior although it still retained its freight carrying capability. It was joined by another C.1 which had previously been operated in Norway on behalf of the C-in-C AFNE. Both Andovers have been transferred to No 60 Squadron.

The Queen's Flight

The Queen's Flight at RAF Benson operates two Westland Wessex HCC.4 to fly members of the Royal Family such as the Queen Mother (seen alighting) whilst on their official duties. Following their RAF training Prince Philip and Prince Charles often take control of the aircraft during their flights.

The Queen's Flight

The BAe 146 became the latest addition to The Queen's Flight when the first of two aircraft was handed over on 23 April 1986. It is the tenth aircraft type designed and built at Hatfield for use by the Royal Family and service with The Queen's Flight, which is also celebrating its 50th anniversary. Designated CC Mk.2 the BAe 146 has been equipped to carry 20 VIP passengers compared with twelve on the Andover CC.2 which it will replace. Besides the seating, it has many capabilities over the Andover: it flies faster—400 knots as against 230 knots; it flies further—1,900 miles as against 1,000 miles; and can fly higher, avoiding most bad weather. The four 6,700 lb Avco Lycoming ALF502 R-3 turbofans will also give a greater margin of safety when operating from marginal airfields, whilst remaining very quiet.

The Queen's Flight

The Queen's Flight has operated three Andover CC.2s from 1964 to fly members of the Royal Family as and when required. The Andover would be used on distances greater than the 200-mile limit of the Wessex although a VC.10 C.1 would be used if the flight were further than 800 miles. Following an evaluation by No 241 OCU, two BAe 146s were ordered for The Queen's Flight. They will eventually replace all but one of the Andovers which will be passed on to No 32 Squadron.

No 41 Squadron

No 41 Squadron at RAF Coltishall is equipped with the Jaguar GR.1 and is now Strike Command's only tactical reconnaissance squadron following the disbanding of the Canberra and Vulcan squadrons. A reconnaissance pod, fitted under the fuselage, carries a range of cameras and sensors to give horizon to horizon coverage. In addition, it carries infra-red linescan to give an all weather capability. The pod is connected to the aircraft's digital computer, enabling it to mark the film with the latitude and longitude. The pilot will also make notes with an event marker should he spot anything while en route or over the target.

Air-to-Air Refuelling

The history of RAF air-to-air refuelling stretches from trials at the Royal Aircraft Establishment Farnborough in 1924 when water was passed down a hose between two Bristol F.2B Fighters, through to the Lockheed Tristar which carries 300,000 lb of fuel plus the support ground crew for the aircraft being deployed.

The RAF interest in air-to-air refuelling was first displayed at RAF Hendon in 1934 but did not really manifest itself until the proving of the 'probe and drogue' technique developed by Sir Alan Chobham's company, Flight Refuelling Ltd, in the late 1940s. Initially, this technique was flown operationally by the Valiants of No 214 Squadron

in the late 1950s, and subsequently joined by No 90 Squadron. With the demise of the Valiant, the Victor took its place.

The first deliveries of the Victor K.1 tankers were made to Nos 55 and 57 Squadrons, followed by No 232 OCU and No 214 Squadron. No 214 Squadron disbanded when the updated K.1As were withdrawn. The other units substituted the K.2 which increased the transferable fuel capacity considerably.

The Victors have been used as a force extender since the mid 1960s, enabling the short range fighters to fly almost anywhere in the world non-stop, typically, from the UK to Cyprus in four and a half hours or the UK to Singapore in a little over fourteen hours. In September 1969, a Victor took part in the first long range interception of a Russian aircraft by an RAF fighter, a role for which they have been kept on quick reaction standby ever since.

Plans were being made to augment the Victor fleet with modified ex-airline VC.10s when the Argentinians invaded the Falkland Islands. The resulting Operation CORPORATE put a massive strain on the tankers, involving them in flying nearly 600 sorties. In addition, Victors were used in the Maritime Radar Reconnaissance (MRR) role in the South Georgia area—so becoming customers for their own Victor tankers. The 'Black Buck' Vulcan missions, which were the longest bombing missions in the history of air warfare, required a fleet of ten Victors for the journey south plus four for the recovery. During each of the fifteen to sixteen-hour missions, some 500,000 lb of fuel was transferred during eighteen night refuellings. A number of Nimrods and Hercules were hastily modified to act as receivers to enable them to operate in the South Atlantic. To try to alleviate some of the strain on the tanker fleet, six Vulcans and six Hercules underwent modification to tankers and, although they were too late to serve in the conflict, they were subsequently used operationally, the Hercules being used extensively in the South Atlantic. Nine Tristars are being modified to tankers in addition to the nine converted VC.10s (five K.2s and four K.3s).

RAF Hercules-to-Hercules aerial refuelling evolved from 'not even considered' to the norm over a matter of weeks. Those crews flying the early missions to Stanley before the airfield was re-opened had a somewhat daunting 8,000-mile round trip, taking anything up to 28 hours. Even Lockheed had not flown a Hercules that long. Once RAF Stanley had been opened, the Air Bridge from Ascension settled down to a Victor K.2 and a Hercules C.1K to provide the fuel for one Hercules C.1P transport making the whole journey. The flight in itself is quite a feat, not least because the bottom speed of the Victor is only just the top speed of the Hercules. The only way that the Hercules can be refuelled safely is by the Victor making a slow descent to allow the Hercules to 'dive' to give the extra margin, starting at about 23,000 ft and completing between 5,000 and 10,000 ft. The Hercules C.1K, having been topped up by the Victor, would then refuel the C.1P half way down to RAF Stanley.

Right: To expedite the conversion of the Hercules into a tanker, some old Andover C.1 long range ferry tanks were brought out of storage. Four of these were fixed to the Hercules' floor, a Hose Drum Unit (HDU) fitted onto the ramp and a hole opened in the ramp for the hose to run out. Whilst this system worked, it was devised in a rush during hostilities and was not considered to be completely safe. As a result the Hercules C.1Ks will return to Marshalls in due course for further modification which will involve the fitting of two larger fuel tanks instead of the four.

Opposite: The hose is streamed out from a Hercules C.1K of No 1312 Flight to another C.1P from No 24 or 30 Squadron somewhere over the South Atlantic.

No 55 Squadron
Despite having been designed by
Handley Page in the late 1940s, the
Victor is still a futuristic looking
aircraft and capable of flying close to
the speed of sound in level flight.
Hawker Siddeley Aviation converted
21 to the tanker role. The two wing
hoses are normally used for refuelling
the smaller fast jet types and the
central hose for the larger aircraft.
This Victor K.2 is from No 55
Squadron and is the last remaining
operator of the type.

No 57 Squadron
A heavily-loaded Victor K.2 from No
57 Squadron rolls at RAF Akrotiri to
position ready for fighters returning
to the UK. The squadron disbanded
on 30 June 1986.

No 101 Squadron

The view from the flight deck of a VC.10 K.3 while it is taking on fuel from another VC.10 tanker. This technique extends the VC.10 tanker's own range and enables it to fly to the best position for its 'chicks' while maintaining the maximum transferrable fuel.

No 216 Squadron

Unable to afford new KC-10s, the Ministry of Defence in 1982 purchased six L1011-500 Tristars from British Airways who were suffering from over capacity. The idea was for Marshalls of Cambridge to convert these aircraft into tankers. In addition, three more Tristars were purchased from Pan Am and these have entered service with No 216 Squadron in the trooping and cargo role.

Above: One of these is seen arriving at RAF Akrotiri to collect troops after an exercise.

Right: Members of the unit parade the Squadron's Standard on 1 November 1984, when No 216 Squadron reformed.

No 11 Group

No 11 Group is responsible for the command and control of the UK Air Defence forces. It currently has two operational squadrons of Lightnings, six squadrons of Phantoms, an Airborne Early Warning (AEW) squadron equipped with the aging Shackleton and two squadrons of Bloodhound surface-to-air missiles. In addition, the Lightning Training Flight and No 229 OCU with Phantoms could be declared as operational squadrons in the event of hostilities. To these are added the Tornado F.2s of No 229 OCU together with those of the operational squadrons as they are re-equipped with the new type. Further reserve aircraft, a number of the Hawks from the Tactical Weapons Units which have been modified to carry the Sidewinder missile, would operate in the inner air defence regions.

No 11 Group maintains a chain of powerful radar stations located throughout the length of UK. These are linked to the NATO Air Defence Grounds Environment (NADGE) which is able to give an early warning of an unidentified aircraft, thus enabling the launch of an interceptor to investigate, identify and escort the aircraft away from UK air space should it be necessary.

The problem with radar is that it can only track in a straight line: it can neither follow the earth's curve over the horizon or undulations in the terrain. Therefore, to avoid detection, current military techniques involve practising flying at very low level. This means that ground radar when placed at sea level is only effective for some 50 miles against low flying aircraft; inland, this distance could well be reduced by any undulations which would create a shadow possibly very close to the radar station. A solution is to move the radar station to a higher elevation, increasing the effective range. If the radar is placed in an aircraft the

No 11 Group, Strike Command—Bentley Priory

No 5 Sqn	Lightning F.3, T.5, F.6	Binbrook
No 8 Sqn	Shackleton AEW.2	Lossiemouth
No 11 Sqn	Lightning F.3, T.5, F.6	Binbrook
No 23 Sqn	Phantom FGR.2	Mount Pleasant
No 25 Sqn		
'A' Flight	Bloodhound	Barkston Heath
'B' Flight	Bloodhound	Wyton (HQ)
'C' Flight	Bloodhound	Wattisham
No 29 Sqn	Phantom FGR.2	Coningsby
No 43 Sqn	Phantom FG.1	Leuchars
No 56 Sqn	Phantom FGR.2	Wattisham
No 63 Sqn (Shadow Sqn for No 2 TWU)	Hawk T.1, T.1A	Chivenor
No 64 Sqn (Shadow Sqn for No 228 OCU)	Phantom FGR.2	Leuchars
No 74 Sqn	Phantom F.3	Wattisham
No 79 Sqn (Shadow Sqn for No 1 TWU)	Hawk T.1, T.1A; Jet Provost T.4	Brawdy
No 85 Sqn		
'A' Flight	Bloodhound	West Raynham (HQ)
'B' Flight	Bloodhound	North Coates
'C' Flight	Bloodhound	Bawdsey
'D' Flight	Bloodhound	West Raynham
No 111 Sqn	Phantom FG.1	Leuchars
No 151 Sqn (Shadow Sqn for No 2 TWU)	Hawk T.1, T.1A	Chivenor
No 234 Sqn (Shadow Sqn for No 1 TWU)	Hawk T.1, T.1A	Brawdy

No 228 OCU	Phantom FGR.2	Leuchars
No 229 OCU	Tornado F.2, F.3	Coningsby
Lightning Augmentation Flight	Lightning F.3, T.5, F.6	Binbrook
Lightning Training Flight	Lightning F.3, T.5	Binbrook
No 1 Tactical Weapons	Hawk T.1, T.1A; Jet Provost T.4	Brawdy
No 2 Tactical Weapons	Hawk T.1, T.1A	Chivenor
Battle of Britain Memorial Flight	Lancaster B. Mk I; Spitfire Mks II; Vb, PR.19; Hurricane Mk IIc; Chipmunk T.10	Coningsby

RAF Regiment

| No 27 Sqn | Rapier | Leuchars |
| No 48 Sqn | Rapier | Lossiemouth |

The EAP

The Experimental Aircraft Programme (EAP) aircraft has been designed and built as a one off prototype to demonstrate and prove the advanced technologies which it is planned to incorporate into the European Fighter Aircraft (EFA). Both aircraft are a collaboration between Britain, Germany, Italy and Spain.

range of the radar increases dramatically. When the RAF assumed the AEW role from the RN Gannets, the last of the Shackletons were modified to carry the same radar sets. They are able to remain flying for much longer periods than the Gannets. The Shackleton was planned as an interim answer pending introduction of NATO's AEW aircraft. However, arguments over the choice of aircraft and splitting of costs of its operation produced a series of delays. With the obsolete Shackleton rapidly reaching the end of its days, the RAF were forced to go ahead on their own. Conversion of eleven of the existing Nimrod maritime reconnaissance aircraft to the AEW role was ordered in 1977 but delays in developing the Marconi multimode, pulse-Doppler radar has embarrassingly stalled their entry into service. This has stretched the life of the Shackleton far beyond that planned. Half of the aircraft have had to be withdrawn as their lives could not be extended further. In hindsight, it would appear that the Boeing E-3 which NATO eventually chose would have been the quicker solution, but, when in service, the Nimrod should be superior for RAF operations in that the system is optimised for over-water operation. This factor will bring much relief to the overworked Shackleton crews whose skill

and effort are the only thing keeping the RAF AEW force functioning. Nevertheless, during 1986, the RAF expressed a preference for the E-3.

Once in service, the No 8 Squadron Nimrod AEW.3s will operate out of RAF Waddington, maintaining two aircraft airborne 24 hours a day, seven days a week. In wartime, a force of four Nimrod AEW.3s flying in a dispersed pattern at 25,000 feet would be able to maintain a constant watch on all the approaches to the UK.

Further radar coverage is made from Fylingdales Ballistic Missile Early Warning System (BMEWS) whose high level radar is able to cover some 3,000 miles across Eastern Europe, giving advance warning of the launch of any intermediate or inter-continental range ballistic missiles. It also tracks satellites and space debris and is networked into the US BMEWS.

At RAF Alconbury, the USAF operates a number of F-5E Tiger IIs in the aggressor role for dissimilar air combat training. With a similar performance to the MiG-21 and pilots trained in Warsaw Pact techniques, the 227th Tactical Fighter Training Aggressor Squadron provides dissimilar combat training not only for USAFE squadrons but also for those of the RAF, especially the interceptors of No 11 Group.

No 5 Squadron
No 5 Squadron is based at RAF Binbrook and is one of the last two Lightning squadrons remaining operational within the RAF. The Lightning entered service with the RAF in 1960 yet it remains a potent interceptor capable of 1,520 mph. The F.6 is the last version built and is fitted with a more advanced radar, navigation and fire control equipment than earlier marks. It is fitted with two 30 mm Aden cannons and would normally carry two Red Top collision-course air-to-air missiles, which are capable of coping with closing speeds of 3,000 mph.

No 11 Squadron

No 11 Squadron is the second of the two Lightning squadrons and is also based at RAF Binbrook. It flies both the F.3 and F.6 in the interceptor role together with a few T.5 dual-control two-seat trainers for continuation training (*below*). The Lightnings are equipped with Red Top air-to-air missiles and two 30 mm Aden cannons. Designed for high level interceptions the Lightning is still a very effective aircraft with a high rate of climb and great speed. Lightning F.6 powered by two of the more powerful Rolls-Royce Avon 301 is capable of accelerating to twice the speed of sound in just three and a half minutes.

Right: Lightning F.6 is fitted with over-wing ferry tanks from which the fuel can be dumped and the empty tanks jettisoned if operational conditions requires immediate return to combat performance.

LAF
All Lightning servicing is carried out at RAF Binbrook. The Lightning Augmentation Flight (LAF) is operated to maintain and hold a reserve of aircraft for the two operational squadrons.

LTF

The Lightning Training Flight (LTF) was formed in 1974 to meet the reducing need for Lightning pilots following the disbanding of No 226 OCU. The Lightning T.5s have a similar performance to that of the single-seat fighter and could be operated by a two-man crew of pilot and weapon system operator. In time of conflict, the LTF would be able to undertake the role of an operational squadron, as would all OCUs.

No 8 Squadron

No 8 Squadron can make the dubious claim to fame of being the operators of the last front-line piston-engined aircraft in the RAF. The Avro Shackleton was designed in the mid 1940s as a maritime reconnaissance aircraft and was flown successfully in this role until the early 1970s when it was replaced by the Nimrod. While this was happening, the RN withdrew the Gannet which had provided the Fleet's airborne early warning coverage. It was realised that the increase in low flying would open a gap in the UK's radar coverage. It was therefore decided to convert twelve of the Shackletons to carry the AN/APS radar sets from the Gannets as an interim measure. Whilst awaiting the introduction of the AEW Nimrod, No 8 Squadron continued to fly the twelve Shackleton AEW.2s but airframe maintenance problems led to the withdrawal of six aircraft. The continued delays have caused numerous problems in keeping aircraft operational, although this has been mainly due to the radar rather than airframe. The location of some twenty new sets in the USA will help to improve the situation.

Eventually, No 8 Squadron may receive the Nimrod AEW.3 and will move to RAF Waddington by which time the old Griffon-engined Shackletons will have retired, so ending another chapter in the RAF's history. However, in the meantime, Shackleton AEW.2s from their base at RAF Lossiemouth still provide an effective cover for maritime surface forces and improve the low level radar cover around the UK through the great skill of the crews from No 8 Squadron.

No 29 Squadron

In 1965, a total of 162 Phantom FGR.2s was ordered for the RAF following the cancellation of the TSR-2, but this was reduced to 116 plus two prototypes. Designated F-4M by McDonnell-Douglas, the RAF Phantom is a development of the US Navy F-4B, including some improvements introduced in the F-4J. When the British Phantoms were ordered, it was stipulated that some 50 per cent of the components were to be manufactured in the UK. The major visible difference between these aircraft and Phantoms flown by other air forces is the replacement of the two General Electric J.79 turbojets with a pair of bulkier Rolls-Royce Spey RB.168-25R Mk 201 series turbofans, each rated at 12,500 lb and having 70 per cent afterburning. This Phantom FGR.2 is flown in the markings of No 29 Squadron from RAF Wattisham, part of the RAF's interceptor force. As such, it would normally carry four Sidewinders and four Sparrow or SkyFlash air-to-air missiles and additional fuel in two underwing tanks and a further tank under the fuselage.

No 23 Squadron

The Phantom FGR.2s of No 23 Squadron were moved to RAF Stanley from RAF Wattisham in 1983. As part of the UK Air Defence Force, No 23 Squadron were well trained in Combat Air Patrols (CAP) and were thus able to take up their duties of providing the air defence for the Falkland Islands on their arrival. The arrival of the Phantoms at RAF Stanley coincided with the opening of the new runway and they were able to relieve the RN Sea Harriers. To facilitate the flying of fully effective CAPs, the Phantoms take advantage of the air-to-air refuelling capability of the Hercules C.1Ks of No 1312 Flight. The opening of RAF Mount Pleasant with the longer runway has meant some improvement in the flying conditions especially since every landing of the Phantoms at RAF Stanley required the use of the arrester landing gear facilities while they can now take off at higher weights.

No 56 Squadron
Taxying back into RAF Wattisham after a CAP training flight is a Phantom FGR.2 of No 56 Squadron. This mission could have taken the crew far out across the North Sea. In-flight refuelling enabled the Phantom to extend its period on patrol.

No 43 Squadron *Opposite top and bottom*

No 43 Squadron, based at RAF Leuchars, flies the Phantom FG.1 which was originally ordered for the Royal Navy in 1964. Designated F-4K by McDonnell-Douglas, it was similar to the FGR.2 but had some modifications specifically for operations from RN aircraft carriers. These included a fixed leading edge slat on the tailplanes, a strengthened main undercarriage and a nose undercarriage leg that could be extended to increase the angle of attack for catapult launches. A total of 59 FG.1s was originally ordered but this was later reduced to 52 aircraft, including prototypes. Initial deliveries went to the RN equipping just one Squadron, but No 43 Squadron reformed in 1969 with the type, as a replacement for the second front line RN squadron that had been planned. In 1978, all remaining FG.1s in the RN were transferred to the RAF due to the run down of the RN's fixedwing fleet.

The more appropriate three-tone grey air defence camouflage scheme (top) has progressively replaced the grey/green scheme. Inherited by the Phantom interceptor squadrons from the tactical squadrons which used the grey/green aircraft until the mid-1970s, it was also standard on the aircraft of No 43 squadron, which was the RAF's only Phantom interceptor squadron until late 1974.

No 64 Squadron (No 228 OCU)
No 64 Squadron is based at RAF
Coningsby and is the 'Shadow
Squadron' of No 228 OCU. Its role is
the conversion of Phantom crews
who come either from No 4 FTS at
RAF Valley via one of the TWUs, or
are transferring from a squadron with
a different aircraft type or are returning to flying from a ground tour. In
time of conflict, No 64 Squadron
would revert to a fully operational
squadron. Also illustrated are some
of the NATO radar jamming pods.

No 74 Squadron *Opposite top and
bottom*
No 74 Squadron reformed during
1984 at RAF Wattisham with the
Phantom F.3. These were ex-US
Navy F-4J Phantoms that were pro-
cured to fill the gap in UKADR left
until the introduction of the Tornado
F.3 by the departure of No 23 Squadron for the South Atlantic. They have
been designated F-4J(UK) by
McDonnell-Douglas and retain their
US equipment to minimise their cost.

No 111 Squadron

No 111 Squadron is based at RAF Leuchars and flies the Phantom FG.1 in the interceptor role and shares the station's 'Q' duties with No 43 Squadron. The RAF Phantoms are normally armed with four Sidewinder plus four Sparrow or SkyFlash AAMs and have a pair of under wing fuel tanks plus another larger one under the fuselage. Normally, only the Phantoms from RAFG fly with the centrally-mounted Vulcan gun pod, but each of the RAF's fighter squadrons visit RAF Akrotiri each year for an Armament Practice Camp (APC) for which the guns are fitted. The M61A1 Vulcan gun is a multi-barrel Gatling gun with a firing rate of some 6,000 rounds of 20 mm ammunition per minute, although the pod has a capacity for only about 1,200 rounds. This formation is flying over the Sovereign Base area of Episkopi and Akrotiri.

Nos 25 and 85 Squadrons

Although the Bloodhound dates back to the mid 1950s, the Mark 2 version which is deployed today is still a highly effective surface-to-air missile, having only recently been updated. Using continuous wave radar in the semi-active guidance system, the Bloodhound Mk 2 is capable of destroying aircraft at ranges up to 80 km and heights of 60,000 ft. The Bloodhound is operated by Nos 25 and 85 Squadrons and flights are deployed at a number of sites along the East Coast.

Maritime Defence

One of the latest additions to the RAF's range of missiles is the Sea Eagle shown here fitted to a Hawk T.1. This missile is a highly sophisticated anti-shipping weapon and it is planned to fit it to the RAF's Tornados and Buccaneers as well as the RN's Sea Harriers.

No 79 Squadron

The British Aerospace Hawk T.1 was designed from the outset as an advanced trainer with a significant ground attack capability, to replace the Hunter. However, in the early 1980s, the Hawk was required to assume a new air defence role, for which 72 have been modified to carry two Sidewinder AAMs and redesignated T.1A. They are painted in the air superiority grey colour scheme. No 79 Squadron is based at RAF Chivenor and is one of the shadow squadrons for No 1 Tactical Weapons Unit (TWU).

No 79 Squadron also operates the Jet Provost T.4 for co-operation work with Forward Air Controllers (FACs) and exchange-posted pilots for familiarisation with RAF operating techniques.

No 234 Squadron

The Hawk is powered by the Rolls-Royce/Turbomeca Adour engine as fitted to the Jaguar, but without re-heat. It is a modular engine and, thus, when a fault develops, only the module affected needs to be replaced. This results in a reduction in the stores holding. Engine access is easy through large doors. Such is the ease of maintenance that the Hawk can easily be turned around in 20 minutes by a single man. Re-arming for weapons training takes four men just 15 minutes. This aircraft is operated by No 234 Squadron from RAF Brawdy and is also part of No 2 TWU.

No 63 Squadron

No 63 Squadron, based at RAF Chivenor, is one of the shadow squadrons of No 1 TWU. As a ground attack trainer, the Hawk T.1 can carry a significant selection of weapons including guns, rockets, bombs and missiles up to a total weight of 5,000 lb spread over its five pylons. Its normal fit is a gun pod under the fuselage and a pair of practice bomb pods under each wing. The raised rear seat gives an excellent view for the instructor, enabling better instruction during the 60 hours' flying on the four-month course.

No 151 Squadron

No 151 Squadron is the second unit of No 2 TWU at RAF Brawdy. The safety record of the Hawk is said by the RAF to be second to none as far as jet aircraft are concerned. Defect rates and maintenance manhours have been dramatically reduced, part of the reason why the Hawk has been so successful. In addition to the 175 ordered for the RAF, Hawks have been ordered by a number of overseas forces including the US Navy.

No 18 Group

Although it is probably best known for its yellow rescue helicopters flying around the British coastline, No 18 Group's main role is the security of the sea lanes around the UK. The Nimrod is the major force within No 18 Group, equipping five squadrons. As the world's first jet maritime reconnaissance aircraft it is able to respond to threats faster and more efficiently than its predecessors. In addition, three Nimrod R.1s are used in the ELINT role by No 51 Squadron. The anti-shipping role is fulfilled by the Buccaneers of Nos 12 and 208 Squadrons whose capabilities will be greatly enhanced by the introduction of the Sea Eagle.

The old Whirlwind which used to be a familiar sight around the British coastline gave way to the Wessex which in turn has been supplanted by the Sea King. Often assisted by the Nimrod, the primary role of the two search and rescue (SAR) squadrons is to rescue RAF aircrew who have had to abandon their aircraft. These duties are controlled to the north of latitude 52° 30′ by the Northern Rescue Control Centre (NRCC) at Pitreavie Castle and to the south by the SRCC at Mount Wise. In practice, their main tasks range from the rescuing of stranded or injured holiday-makers to mercy flights. Each year, the crews are responsible for saving the lives of hundreds of people, often endangering their own lives in doing so.

No 18 Group also retains a few Canberras with No 100 Squadron, for target duties in various roles, and No 360 Squadron, whose ugly looking T.17s are used as a radar and ECM source for training a wide range of personnel in the techniques of operating in the hostile electronic environment. No 1 PRU uses the remaining Canberra PR.9s for aerial survey work and No 231 OCU is responsible for training new aircrew before they join one of the squadrons.

No 18 Group, Strike Command—Northwood

Unit	Aircraft	Base
No 12 Sqn	Buccaneer S.2B	Lossiemouth
No 22 Sqn		
HQ	Wessex HC.2	Finningley
'A' Flight	Wessex HC.2	Chivenor
'B' Flight	Wessex HC.2	Leuchars
'C' Flight	Wessex HC.2	Valley
'D' Flight	Wessex HC.2	Leconfield
'E' Flight	Wessex HC.2	Manston
No 42 Sqn	Nimrod MR.2*	St Mawgan
No 51 Sqn	Nimrod R.1	Wyton
No 100 Sqn	Canberra B.2, PR.7, E.15, TT.18	Wyton
No 120 Sqn	Nimrod MR.2**	Kinloss
No 201 Sqn	Nimrod MR.2**	Kinloss
No 202 Sqn		
HQ	Sea King HAR.3	Finningley
'A' Flight	Sea King HAR.3	Boulmer
'B' Flight	Sea King HAR.3	Brawdy
'C' Flight	Sea King HAR.3	Coltishall
'D' Flight	Sea King HAR.3	Lossiemouth
No 206 Sqn	Nimrod MR.2**	Kinloss
No 208 Sqn	Buccaneer S.2A, S.2B	Lossiemouth
No 360 Sqn	Canberra T.17	Wyton
No 231 OCU	Canberra T.4	Wyton
No 236 OCU	Nimrod MR.2*	St Mawgan
No 237 OCU	Buccaneer S.2A, Hunter T.7	Honington

*of St Mawgan Nimrod Wing.   **of Kinloss Nimrod Wing.*

No 1 PRU	Canberra PR.9	Wyton
Search and Rescue Training Flight	Wessex HC.2	Valley
Sea King Training Unit	Sea King HAR.3	Culdrose

Royal Auxiliary Air Force Maritime HQ

No 1 (County of Hertford) Sqn	Northwood
No 2 (County of Edinburgh) Sqn	Pitreavie Cast
No 3 (County of Devon) Sqn	Mount Batten

No 12 Squadron

The Blackburn Buccaneer was originally designed for RN requirements as a two-seat strike/attack/reconnaissance aircraft. With the cancellation of the TSR.2, followed by that of its replacement, the F-111K, the RAF was left without a high-speed strike aircraft so 43 Buccaneer S.2Bs were ordered from Hawker Siddeley. The Buccaneer was optimised for low-level operations, and the RAF now possessed a potent weapon and later ordered three more. In addition, with the run down of the RN fixed-wing fleet, all the remaining Buccaneers were transferred to the RAF.

In 1969, No 12 Squadron became the first RAF squadron to fly the Buccaneer. Now based at RAF Lossiemouth, it flies in the maritime strike role, for which its aircraft are usually equipped with the Martel air-to-surface missile, which is in the process of being replaced by the Sea Eagle. They can also carry 1,000 lb iron, cluster or laser-guided bombs and nuclear weapons. The Buccaneer is fitted with four pylons which can carry up to three 1,000 lb bombs and has an internal rotating bomb bay which can carry additional weapons.

No 208 Squadron

No 208 Squadron is the second operational No 18 Group Buccaneer squadron and has now joined No 12 Squadron in the maritime strike role, having previously flown overland interdiction. As it was originally designed for RN operations, the Buccaneer has a number of folding features, including the wings, nose and tail cone. Although these features are not used in RAF operation, the folding tail cone doubles as a highly effective airbrake. In addition to its offensive role, the Buccaneer also acts as a tanker, carrying the HDU in its bomb bay. In this role, it would probably escort another Buccaneer or a Tornado to provide refuelling where a conventional tanker would be too vulnerable.

No 237 OCU

The Buccaneer training unit is No 237 OCU which is also based at RAF Lossiemouth alongside the two operational squadrons. It uses the Buccaneer S.2A, which is the ex-RN version and has not been converted for Martel operations, for the 75-hour crew conversion course. Following the discovery of metal fatigue in 1982, a number of Buccaneers were scrapped and they were withdrawn from RAFG and replaced by the Tornado. However, those that have been cleared will stay in service until the 1990s, remaining highly effective through updates to the ECM and navigation packages.

Nimrod

The Hawker Siddeley Nimrod was designed around the well-proven Comet 4C airframe, with the addition of a large pannier under the fuselage to carry weapons and the new radar. ESM is housed in a fairing on the fin tip plus a Magnetic Anomaly Detector (MAD) boom extends from the rear and a 70 million candlepower searchlight on the wing fuel tank. A total of 46 Nimrods was ordered for the anti-submarine warfare/maritime reconnaissance (ASW/MR) roles, plus three for electronic intelligence (ELINT) purposes with No 51 Squadron.

Power is supplied by four 12,500 lb Rolls-Royce Spey 250 turbojets, enabling the Nimrod to transit to the search area at speeds in excess of 400 knots and an altitude of about 30,000 ft—much faster than any of its contemporaries. Once near the search area, the Nimrod slows down and descends to its operational height, which can be as low as 100 ft and two engines are shut down to give the optimum fuel consumption and endurance. The internal equipment is then used to detect the target. Such is the power to weight ratio that, if required, the Nimrod could still climb on one engine when operating at normal search weights.

Inside the Nimrod, the flight deck follows the basic Comet layout but with updated instruments. The real changes are aft of these positions. Only eleven of the Comet-style windows have been retained but three bubble windows have been added for the Mark 1 Eyeballs of the observers. When required, the bubble windows can be opened in flight to facilitate photography of suspected targets. In the main fuselage, the rest of the crew of twelve man positions according to the phase of operation and the nature of the task. As the effectiveness of the Nimrod depends on the correct harmony of the airframe, equipment and crew, much thought was devoted to maximising the effectiveness of each.

A wide range of equipment is fitted in the Nimrod to assist in the detection, identification and location of surface vessels and submarines. Air to surface (ASV) radar is used to detect surface shipping and periscopes or snorkels. Electronic Support Measures (ESM) in the fin tip aerial detects and locates any source of radar transmissions. An ionisation detector in the nose is able to 'sniff' the atmosphere and detect and track diesel-powered submarines' exhaust emissions.

A sonar system provides accurate short-range location and tracking using active and passive sonobuoys. An On-Top-Position-Indicator gives a precise indication of passage over operating sonobuoys. The MAD equipment indicates the presence of a submerged vessel from the disturbance of the earth's magnetic field created by the vessel. Once the crew have positively identified an enemy vessel, the Nimrods can attack it with air-droppable torpedoes. During the Falklands campaign, the Nimrods were fitted with probes enabling them to take advantage of in-flight refuelling. These aircraft were designated Nimrod MR.2P. During the period of operations in the Falklands, over 150 missions were flown, including one which lasted nineteen hours. In addition, the aircraft were modified to enable them to carry the Harpoon anti-ship missile, Sting Ray torpedoes and, for self defence, Sidewinder missiles.

In 1974, security flights began around the British coastline, basically to survey the oil rigs but included fishery protection. The flights are known as Offshore Tapestry. The establishment of a 200-mile Exclusive Economic Zone in 1977 requires an area of 180,000 square miles to be surveyed.

The Nimrod MR.2 has been updated and carries the Searchwater system, the world's most advanced computerised radar. It is able to identify by name any vessel that it detects by comparing the vessel's characteristics with records stored in its memory.

In 1977, an order was placed with British Aerospace to convert eleven of the Nimrods for the AEW role. Externally, these aircraft differ dramatically from the standard Nimrod due to the addition of radar dishes in enlarged radomes at the nose and tail.

The RAF's Maritime Nimrod force is split between RAF Kinloss, with Nos 120, 201 and 206 Squadrons, in the North and RAF St Mawgan in the South, with No 42 Squadron and No 237 OCU.

An important part of the Nimrod system is the radar of which the scanner is visible and is capable of spotting a submarine periscope in a rough sea. This capability is also very useful in the SAR role for locating anybody in distress.

Nimrods from the Central Servicing Wing ready for flight on the flight line at RAF Kinloss.

The cockpit of the Nimrod is basically similar to that of the de Havilland Comet 4C, from which the aircraft was developed.

Opposite
A Nimrod displays its capacious weapons bay. The Nimrod is fitted with a remotely-controlled 70 million candle power lamp on the front of the wing pod, enabling the crew to make visual search at night.

The Nimrods are being fitted with extra pods on the wing tips containing LORAL ESM, equipment to give warning-analysis of hostile radar.

No 100 Squadron

No 100 Squadron at RAF Wyton flies the Canberra on target facility duties for all three services. As the Canberra has gradually been withdrawn, the squadron has managed to acquire a variety of remainders of the different marks, including B.2, PR.7, E.15 and TT.18. The B.2 and E.15 are usually used for practical training of fighter ground controllers whilst the PR.7 and TT.1B are used for towing targets for live gunnery or air-to-air missile training. This Canberra illustrated is an E.15.

No 360 Squadron

Based at RAF Wyton, No 360 Squadron flies the Canberra T.17. This version of the 1950s bomber has been heavily modified to enable it to operate in the electronic counter measure (ECM) role. It is somewhat unique for an RAF Squadron in that it is 25 per cent funded and manned by the RN. The facilities provided by the Canberra T.17s of No 360 Squadron are used to provide ECM training for army, navy and air force personnel, and the aircraft take part in all UK and NATO exercises.

No 231 OCU

Despite having entered service in 1951, the English Electric Canberra still fulfils a valuable role for the RAF and in addition serves with the RN at RNAS Yeovilton. As sufficient aircraft are still flying to require fresh crews No 231 OCU continues its association with the Canberra, having formed on the type in 1949. It operates alongside the remaining three squadrons at RAF Wyton and is equipped with the dual-control T.4 version.

Search & Rescue

SARTF *Left*
The Search And Rescue Training Flight (SARTF) is based at RAF Valley and operates the Wessex HC.2 for the training of aircrew in the skills and disciplines involved in airborne search and rescue. This Wessex HC.2 was photographed in an interim colour scheme shortly after its delivery from an operational squadron to SARTF before it received the overall yellow colour scheme.

No 22 Squadron *Above*
No 22 Squadron flies the Wessex HC.2 from a number of detached flights around the British coast. At each of the flights, one helicopter is kept on a fifteen-minute standby during daylight hours or one hour at night for 365 days a year. Powered by a pair of Rolls-Royce Gnome turbines, the Wessex has a maximum range of 290 miles but is restricted to a maximum payload of 3,600 lb.

Although this is an improvement over the Whirlwind it does suffer from insufficient power especially when flying in poor conditions. The Wessex is normally crewed by a pilot, a navigator and a winchman.

SKTF

The Sea King Training Flight (SKTF) formed at RNAS Culdrose with the assistance of No 706 Squadron, Fleet Air Arm, using the first of the RAF's Sea King HAR.3s. Its purpose was and is to train crews in SAR techniques for No 202 Squadron. The forming of No 1564 Flight at Stanley in the Falkland Islands created additional requirements. The flight trains on average eighteen crew members per year, including pilots, navigators and winchmen.

The Sea King HAR.3 would normally carry fifteen survivors but could manage 22 in an emergency in addition to the four crew. The Sea King has an unrefuelled radius of action of 270 miles—almost double that of the Wessex—and could operate for four hours if refuelled en route from oil platforms or using the Helicopter In Flight Refuelling (HIFR) system whereby the Sea King would drop a fuel line and obtain fuel from a ship while hovering overhead.

No 202 Squadron

No 202 Squadron has its headquarters at RAF Finningley but has a number of flights around the UK roughly alternating with the Wessex flights of No 22 Squadron. No 202 Squadron flies the Sea King HAR.3 of which sixteen were originally ordered but an additional three were added later to replace those in the South Atlantic.

A Sea King HAR.3 is kept at fifteen minutes readiness at each of the flights during daylight and 45 minutes at night. However, the helicopters of both Nos 22 and 202 Squadrons are normally airborne well within these times. On hearing of the Air India disaster off Eire in 1985, the first Sea King from No 202 Squadron's 'B' Flight at RAF Brawdy was airborne within a couple of minutes and all three helicopters from the flight were en route within 48 minutes due to a tremendous effort by everybody concerned. Such was the scale of the accident that they were joined by another RAF Sea King as well as RN Sea Kings and Chinooks from No 7 Squadron.

No 78 Squadron

The Sea King HAR.3s of No 1564 Flight had been based on the Falklands since shortly after the islands were liberated from Argentinian occupation. Located at Naval Point close to Stanley, No 1564 Flight provided the same SAR cover as Nos 22 and 202 Squadrons in the UK. However, because the Argentinians have failed to declare a cease-fire, the British forces remain on alert. It is therefore inappropriate for the Sea Kings to be painted in their usual bright yellow as they would become easy targets. For this reason, each of the Sea Kings of No 1564 Flight was painted in a grey colour scheme. In 1986, the flight merged with the Chinooks of No 1310 Flight to become No 78 Squadron. Crews rotate from No 202 Squadron on four-month tours during which they can fly in excess of a year's normal UK flying hours. Besides their SAR role, numerous additional tasks are flown which include not only medivac and casevac but also carrying troops and freight. The Sea Kings are also used for ground support, during which a general purpose machine gun (GPMG) may be fitted, and for fighter affiliation.

No 51 Squadron *Opposite*

No 51 Squadron is also based at RAF Wyton and is equipped with three specially modified Nimrods which are designated R.1. These are distinguishable from the other Nimrods because they have no MAD sting at the tail and have numerous aerials. They are used by the RAF for gathering electronic intelligence (ELINT).

No 1 PRU

No 1 Photo Reconnaissance Unit (PRU) is the last operator of the Canberra PR.9. Based at RAF Wyton, it has five aircraft on its strength and uses them to carry out various aerial survey tasks mainly for map making. This role demands extremely accurate flying, but the Canberra PR.9 was specially designed as a highly-stable platform and is capable of performing at high levels with long range and endurance. Flown by a crew of two, the pilot and navigator have to ensure that the correct track, altitude and attitude are flown to ensure that no gaps in coverage of the terrain appear when the photographs are pieced together. Besides taking survey quality photographs, the Canberra PR.9 can also carry the infrared Linescan equipment which is so sensitive that it can even locate sources of lost heat in underground heating pipes.

Overseas Bases

Belize		
No 1417 Flight	Harrier GR.3	Belize City Apt.
No 1563 Flight	Puma HC.1	Belize City Apt.
	Rapier	Belize City Apt.

Cyprus		
No 84 Sqn	Wessex HU.5	Akrotiri
No 34 Sqn, RAF Regt	Light Armour	Akrotiri

Falklands		
No 23 Sqn	Phantom FGR.2	Mount Pleasant
No 78 Sqn	Chinook HC.1; Sea King HAR.3	Mount Pleasant
No 1312 Flight	Hercules C.1K	Mount Pleasant

Hong Kong		
No 28 Sqn	Wessex HC.2	Sek Kong

No 28 Squadron

No 28 Squadron is the last remnant of the RAF's Far East Air Force (FEAF) and is based at RAF Sek Kong in Hong Kong. This is an extremely busy unit, contributing to the ground forces continual task of intercepting the thousands of illegal immigrants trying to reach Hong Kong from mainland China. It also provides air mobility for the Army observation posts placed around the Colony. These Wessex are flying over the Mai Po marshes while deploying troops. The Wessex HC.2s of No 28 Squadron have white stripes painted around the rear fuselage to make them more visible to other pilots.

No 84 Squadron

No 84 Squadron is based at RAF Akrotiri and operates ex-RN Wessex HU.5s, which replaced its obsolete Whirlwinds. It serves two roles: flying in support of the United Nations peace-keeping forces in Cyprus, and flying SAR duties. In 1984, No 84 Squadron operated as Britain's contribution in support of the multinational force in Lebanon. Visible at the bottom of the picture is Princess Mary's Hospital at RAF Akrotiri.

MATO

Military Air Traffic Operations (MATO) has a Group Status within Strike Command. It is co-located with the Civil Air Traffic Operations at Uxbridge where a Joint Field Commander is responsible for the combined implementation of the National Air Traffic Services policy for the control of civil and military aircraft in the UK. Housed inside the Control Tower, the controllers of RAF Brize Norton provide assistance to any aircraft within their zone.

RAF Germany

Royal Air Force Germany (RAFG), which has its headquarters at Rheindahlen, operates a sizeable portion of the RAF's front line strength. This is a descendant from 2TAF of World War Two. It is tasked with fulfilling, in the air, Britain's responsibilities under the Bonn Accords, which include:

in peace time, under responsibilities retained by the United Kingdom pending the conclusion of a German peace treaty and in close integration with NATO, the defence of the integrity of the airspace of the northern half of the Federal Republic of Germany and, with the United States Air Force and the French Air Force, the maintenance of access to Berlin in the three air corridors.

The RAF's commitment is achieved by two squadrons of Phantom FGR.2s whose task is to police the northern half of the 30-mile wide Air Defence Identification Zone. This buffer zone runs the length of the East German border to prevent infringements by either side of national airspace. An intruding Flogger would only take fifteen minutes to reach RAF Gutersloh and 30 minutes to Rheindahlen and the 'clutch' airfields of RAF Laarbruch, Bruggen and Wildenrath.

RAFG is completely autonomous in peacetime, reporting directly to the Ministry of Defence through its Commander-in-Chief. In addition to the two interceptor squadrons, a further twelve squadrons complete the UK's commitment to NATO's Second Allied Tactical Air Force (2ATAF). These squadrons provide conventional ground attack, nuclear strike and reconnaissance in support of any NATO operation. Until recently, four of the squadrons were equipped with Jaguars and two with Buccaneers but both these types have been replaced by the Tornado GR.1. One squadron of Jaguars remains at RAF Laarbruch in the reconnaissance role but this will also re-equip with Tornados in due course.

Two squadrons of Harriers, a Puma squadron and a Chinook squadron are based at RAF Gutersloh to support the Army's 1 (Br) Corps. They could, however, also be made available if required to support 2ATAF. At RAF Wildenrath, a communication squadron which operates the last of the RAF's Pembrokes is now overdue for re-equipment and will shortly receive Andovers. At Berlin, Gatow Station Flight flies two Chipmunks to exercise the RAF's rights to operate aircraft over Berlin's British sector under the Treaty arrangements.

To reduce the vulnerability of the airfields, a comprehensive programme of toning down and hardening of structures and surroundings plus important buildings has been undertaken, making the airfields more difficult to locate from the air and less vulnerable to air weapons. No longer are lines of aircraft to be seen on aprons: all the strike aircraft are now protected, one or two at a time, in a bomb resistant Hardened Aircraft Shelter (HAS) in which the aircraft can be refuelled, serviced, re-armed and started with the large armoured doors still closed. After making pre-flight checks, the doors are opened to allow the aircraft to taxi out to the end of the runway and take off on a mission with a minimum of vulnerable exposure. Each HAS is positioned so that an attacking aircraft would be unable to knock out more than one such structure in a single pass.

The capabilities of the Tornado mean that it could still operate from taxiways should the main runways be damaged. Despite all of these precautions, RAFG airfields would be a primary target in time of conflict and, therefore, there would be some successful attacks. Vital runways and taxiways might be hit and so each airfield has a large stock of gravel and other materials with which to effect quick repairs. One or two Gazelle HT.3s from RAF Shawbury would be detached to each airfield to allow quick assessment of battle damage and to give priority for the Royal Engineer Airfield Damage Repair Squadrons. Their aim is for a troop to be able to repair two craters within two and a half hours.

Each of the airfields has its own Rapier-equipped RAF Regiment squadron for protection against attacking enemy aircraft. At present the RAF Regiment Rapier squadrons are gaining a great deal of operational experience during detachments to the Falkland Islands.

To disperse further the vulnerability of valuable aircraft, the Harriers regularly operate from rough strips away from base. In recent years, the Jaguars have had exercises using the autobahns as runways and this capability has also been demonstrated recently with a Tornado.

Having strengthened and toned down the airfields for protection from air attack, there remains the problem of protection from ground attack. The RAF Regiment has one unit, No 1 Squadron, based at RAF Laarbruch to protect the Harrier squadrons but No 33 Wing Headquarters at RAF Gutersloh could call upon four RAF Regiment squadrons from the UK and another from Cyprus. These squadrons are equipped with Scorpion and Spartan armoured vehicles.

Besides its operational squadrons, RAF Bruggen houses No 431 MU which is responsible for all second line servicing of RAFG aircraft. In the event of tension it would deploy its personnel and as much kit as possible around the four main RAFG airfields.

No 2 FTS

In time of war, the Gazelle HT.1s of No 2 FTS from RAF Shawbury would be used by the operational RAFG stations for quick battle damage assessment after an enemy attack. This would enable the ground units to undertake urgent repairs in order of priority to enable those aircraft already airborne to return to base after their missions and those on the ground to take to the air as soon as they are required.

RAF Germany—Rheindahlen

Strike/Attack

No 9 Sqn	Tornado GR.1	Bruggen
No 15 Sqn	Tornado GR.1	Laarbuch
No 16 Sqn	Tornado GR.1	Laarbuch
No 14 Sqn	Tornado GR.1	Bruggen
No 17 Sqn	Tornado GR.1	Bruggen
No 31 Sqn	Tornado GR.1	Bruggen

Ground Support

No 3 Sqn	Harrier GR.3, T.4	Gutersloh
No 4 Sqn	Harrier GR.3, T.4	Gutersloh

Reconnaissance

No 2 Sqn	Jaguar G.R.1, T.2	Laarbuch

Air Defence

No 19 Sqn*	Phantom FGR.2	Wildenrath
No 92 Sqn*	Phantom FGR.2	Wildenrath

Communications

No 60 Sqn	Andover C.1; Pembroke C.1	Wildenrath
Berlin Station Flight	Chipmunk T.10	Berlin/Gatow

Air Transport

No 18 Sqn	Chinook HC.1	Gutersloh
No 230 Sqn	Puma HC.1	Wildenrath

Support

No 431 Maintenance Unit	—	Bruggen

* Declared to NATO Command Forces.

RAF Regiment

HQ No. 33 Wing

No 1 Sqn	Light Armour	Laarbruch

HQ No. 4 Wing

No 16 Sqn	Rapier	Wildenrath
No 26 Sqn	Rapier	Laarbruch
No 37 Sqn	Rapier	Bruggen
No 63 Sqn	Rapier	Gutersloh

Royal Engineers

Nos 48, 50, 52 and 53 Sqns	Field Construction

No 2 Squadron

No 2 Squadron, based at RAF Laarbruch, is the last remaining RAFG Jaguar unit following the conversion of No 14 Squadron to Tornados in 1985. Whilst all of the previous Jaguar squadrons flew their aircraft in the strike/attack role, No 2 Squadron operates as a tactical reconnaissance unit. All the airborne equipment required for this role is fitted in a pod carried under the Jaguar's fuselage.

No 3 Squadron

No 3 Squadron is based at RAF Gutersloh from where it operates the Harrier GR.3 in the close support role. Its unique vertical/short take-off capability enables the Harrier to operate from almost anywhere. It can thus be based very close to the battle area, resulting in very fast reactions to requests for close air support from Army commanders. The Harrier has a fast rate of climb, reaching 10,000 feet in less than 40 seconds, although it is more likely to fly at low level for its operational missions. It can also fly at speeds up to Mach 0.95 in level flight. It usually carries two 30 mm Aden cannons in pods under the fuselage and has provision to carry up to 5,000 lb of ordnance on four underwing pylons plus one under the fuselage. These stores might include free-fall or retarded bombs, or cluster bomb units, rocket pods and flares.

To enable the Harriers to operate from unprepared sites without being too exposed to enemy reconnaissance, they are usually parked in camouflaged hides. With its in-built auxiliary power unit, which supplies all essential electrical power, it can remain at a high state of readiness with a minimum of support equipment.

No 4 Squadron

No 4 Squadron also operates Harriers from RAF Gutersloh in close support of 1 (BR) Corps. As with all of the Harrier units, No 4 Squadron frequently deploys away from its base on exercises, often to semi-prepared sites. Also in line with other Harrier units, No 4 Squadron is equipped with the Harrier T.4 dual-control two-seat trainer as well as the single-seat GR.3. The two-seat Harrier is used for various facets of pilot training and refresher training. It has a similar performance and weapons carrying capabilities to the GR.3 and would be flown operationally on the same sorties as the GR.3 in time of war. The comprehensive navigation and attack system, which lays special emphasis on high-speed, low-level operations, shows the pilot his position by means of an optically-projected moving map display.

No XV Squadron

No XV Squadron is based at RAF Laarbruch and flies the Tornado GR.1. Previously flying the Buccaneer, the Tornado re-equipping pro gramme became urgent when fatigue problems caused the Buccaneer fleet to be temporarily grounded and a number of the aircraft had to be scrapped. In this picture the Tornado to the left is fitted with 1,000 lb general purpose bombs under the fuselage while the other aircraft in the HAS is fitted with two JP233 area denial pods. The latter can be fitted with a range of cratering submunitions for breaking up runways and taxiways and a mixture of anti-personnel and anti-repair vehicle mines plus additional ones fitted with timers to give random explosions, thus deterring any repairs to damaged areas.

No 14 Squadron

No 14 Squadron is the last of the RAFG strike units to re-equip with the Tornado GR.1 in place of the previously flown Jaguar GR.1. This aircraft is fitted with seven ALARM (Air Launched Anti-Radiation Missiles) and, although a maximum of nine may be fitted if the Tornado is on radar suppression, it is more likely that four missiles would be fitted in pairs in the inboard wing pylons. The Tornado would then be able to carry a normal weapons load, giving it the additional capability to suppress enemy radar en route, thus making its detection and destruction very difficult. ALARM has two modes. In the direct attack mode, it flies straight at the radar, as with many other such weapons. Where it is unique is the indirect mode. The easy defence for the radar operator is to turn off the radar until the missile has passed but ALARM uses its rocket motor to climb to some 40,000 feet, deploy a parachute and then re-assess the target situation, and to attack any further emissions according to a programmed order of priority. By this time, the Tornado would be well out of range.

No 16 Squadron

No 16 Squadron, like No XV, is based at RAF Laarbruch and was previously flying the Buccaneer until it was urgently replaced by the Tornado GR.1. The Tornado GR.1 is powered by the Rolls-Royce RB199 Mk 103 turbofan which gives 9,656 lb thrust dry, increasing to 16,920 lb with full afterburner as seen in this fiery evening shot.

No 17 Squadron *Left*
No 17 Squadron gave up its Jaguars in 1985 for the Tornado GR.1 which it flies from RAF Bruggen. The Tornado is the product of much international co-operation between the British, German and Italian partners. Although each country has its own final assembly line, the sub-assemblies are not duplicated. Each member of the Panavia consortium is responsible for the production of its respective sections which are then distributed to the three final assembly lines. The value of this production split is in proportion to the number of aircraft ordered by the respective

Governments, the British building the cockpit and tail, Germans building the mid-fuselage and the extreme nose and tail, and the Italians producing the wings. The additional orders for the Omani and Saudi air forces will be satisfied relatively quickly by jumping the production queue and taking some of the aircraft designated for the RAF. Although this would appear to delay the RAF's re-equipment programme, the RAF's pilot shortage problem will allow further crews to be trained ready for the later delivery off the production line.

No 20 Squadron *Above*
Based at RAF Laarbruch, No 20 Squadron replaced its Jaguars with the Tornado GR.1 in 1984. All RAFG strike aircraft, with the exception of the Harriers, are now placed in Hardened Aircraft Shelters (HAS) which are designed to protect the aircraft from air attack. Positioned so that an attacking aircraft would be unable to hit more than one aircraft, the HAS are so equipped that each is a self contained unit capable of housing, repairing, refuelling and re-arming either one or two aircraft. Such is the air conditioning that the Tornado may be started inside the HAS before the doors are opened. Gone are the days of lines of aircraft on the pans ready for their flight.

No 31 Squadron

No 31 Squadron is based at RAF Bruggen and has flown the Tornado GR.1 since it relinquished its Jaguars in 1985. The forward locations of the RAFG Tornados would enable them to hit targets in the Warsaw Pact countries of East Germany, Poland, Czechoslovakia, Hungary and even just into the USSR, but this range could be increased for deeper strikes through the use of buddy refuelling from another Tornado or possibly Buccaneers.

No 18 Squadron

RAFG's heavy lift capability is supplied by the Chinook HC.1s of No 18 Squadron, based at RAF Gutersloh. Along with the Harriers and Pumas the squadron frequently operates in the field on exercises with 1 (BR) Corps. With many unique capabilities the Chinook can carry loads far in excess of previous RAF helicopters. This would give 1 (Br) Corps the necessary support to be able to match a potentially fast moving adversary.

No 19 Squadron
A Phantom FGR.2 of No 19 Squadron being pushed back into its HAS at RAF Wildenrath after a sortie. RAFG Phantoms normally fly sorties in conjunction with ground radar or a NATO E-3A Sentry flying radar station. The crews are also trained to be autonomous so that should the control stations cease to function, the Phantoms could still continue to track and destroy intruders.

No 92 Squadron
The Phantom FGR.2s of No 92 Squadron are also based at RAF Wildenrath, operating with No 19 Squadron in the interceptor role. Aircraft are maintained permanently on Quick Reaction Alert (QRA) or 'Q' for short, by the Battle Flight. When the klaxons wail a Phantom is scrambled and roars down the runway and is then directed by the ground radar until it is able to track the intruder in the buffer zone for itself. Although this happens several times a week, until now the culprit has been found to be an off-track civil aircraft or an airliner with a faulty transponder, but each and every case is checked just in case!

No 60 Squadron

The Pembroke C.1 is still used by No 60 Squadron at RAF Wildenrath as a communications aircraft. Originally built by Hunting in the mid 1950s, the Pembroke saw service with eleven squadrons and various flights. Unfortunately, it was found to be suffering from metal fatigue in the wing spar and most were withdrawn, but in 1970 a decision was made to re-spar fourteen aircraft due to the lack of a suitable replacement. No 60 Squadron is the last RAF unit to fly the Pembroke although these have been augmented with Andover C.1s.

No 230 Squadron

No 230 Squadron operates the Puma HC.1 from RAF Gutersloh and, like the other residing squadrons flying the Harriers and Chinook, spends much of its time operating away from base on exercises with 1 (Br) Corps. Forty Pumas were originally ordered for the RAF but a further eight were ordered to replace attrition losses.

Berlin SF
The RAF have two Chipmunk T.10s
based at RAF Gatow where they
regularly fly to exercise the Royal Air
Force's right to fly over Berlin as part
of the 1945 Treaty obligations.

RAF Support Command

RAF Support Command was formed on 13 June 1977 by the merger of two existing RAF Commands—Training and Support. Based at RAF Brampton in Cambridgeshire, the merger produced a simple three Command structure providing a more efficient and cost effective back up for the Strike and RAF Germany Commands.

In addition to being responsible for the RAF College at Cranwell, the RAF Staff College at Bracknell and the HQ Air Cadets at RAF Newton, RAF Support Command contains two main function groups—one to give the necessary training to all officers and airmen, and the second to maintain equipment beyond the day to day capabilities of operational stations.

Through the Air Training Corps (ATC) and the RAF sections of the Combined Cadet Force (CCF), RAF Support Command encourages young people from thirteen to twenty years old to have an interest in aviation and provides them with some basic training in both service and civilian life. Through some 900 squadrons, approximately 45,000 young boys and girls are able to experience flying in gliders and powered aircraft at the thirteen Air Experience Flights (AEF) and 27 Gliding Schools. On leaving school, those who wish to join the Royal Air Force have initially two options, a direct entry as an officer or an airman or to continue further education at a university. Approximately 25 per cent of officers and airmen are provided by Air Cadets, including 40 per cent of aircrew.

Of those selecting direct entry, some 1,200 potential officers are accepted annually through the Officer and Aircrew Selection Centre at RAF Biggin Hill. Those successful then spend eighteen months at the RAF College at Cranwell before joining their specialist courses. In addition, about 7,500 men and women enter the RAF through the Recruit Training School at RAF Swinderby with a six-week basic training course. These airmen and airwomen then progress to specialist training in one of 150 separate trades.

The trade training is largely engineering biased and is mainly carried out at the RAF training schools at Cosford, Halton, Locking and St Athan. A further school at RAF Hereford provides General Service Training later in their careers for airmen and airwomen selected for possible promotion to corporal and sergeants. Annually, approximately 20,000 service men and women attend around 680 different ground courses, which can range from under a week to a three-year apprenticeship. In addition, some 1,500 civilians are given technical and management training.

For the students who leave school and are interested in joining the RAF but would like to continue their education through university, there is the opportunity to join one of the sixteen University Air Squadrons (UAS). Parented by RAFC Cranwell, the purpose of the UAS is to encourage the cadet's motivation and develop them as junior officers. In addition, they provide basic flying training for potential aircrew in Bulldogs as well as flying experience for those wishing to enter one of the other branches.

Following Initial Officer Training, most potential pilots spend fourteen hours flying Chipmunks at the Flying Selection Squadron at RAF Swinderby. Here, they are assessed for their suitability before commencing their basic flying training on Jet Provosts at RAFC Cranwell, No 7 FTS at RAF Church Fenton or No 1 FTS at RAF Linton-on-Ouse. During this part of their training the pilots are selected for their next stream of advanced training—fast jet, multiple engine or helicopter. Fast jet pilots destined for air defence or ground attack go to RAF Valley and fly Hawks, the multi-engine crews go to RAF Finningley to fly Jet-streams and the helicopter pilots to RAF Shaw-bury, with Gazelles and Wessex. On completion of their respective courses, each of the pilots are presented with their Wings before progressing on to Strike Command and an operational conversion unit (OCU) where they are trained on the aircraft type that they will fly at squadron level. In addition, Support Command provides a twenty-week fixed-wing flying course for all RN pilots at the Royal Navy Elementary Flying Training Squadron (RNEFTS), with Bulldogs.

Training of all the other aircrew is carried out at RAF Finningley. On completion of their ground training, all navigators gain experience in Dominies and Jet Provosts, while air engineers and electronics operators use the Dominies. RAF Scampton now houses the Central Flying School (CFS). Its function is to train flying instructors for all three services as well as for a number of overseas nations.

Once through the Initial Officer Training, those officers bound for the ground branch then progress to their respective schools—engineering and supply at RAFC Cranwell, Air Traffic Control (ATC) at RAF Shawbury, secretarial at RAF Hereford, catering at Aldershot and police and education at RAF Newton. Later in their service life there are further courses at RAF Henlow and the Staff College at Bracknell.

RAF Support Command's other main role is maintaining aircraft, signals, supply and engineering. Engineering support is provided by Support Command for all RAF aircraft plus the fixed-wing aircraft of the Army and RN. Scheduled major servicing, rectification, reconditioning and modification tasks that are beyond the capabilities of squadrons or station level are undertaken on all aircraft by maintenance units (MU). These MU also hold reserve stocks of fixed-wing aircraft but, due to the extremely high cost of each aircraft, requirements dictate that they should be fully serviceable and operational for the maximum part of their service life.

The MU at RAF Kemble now supports USAFE aircraft, leaving RAF Abingdon and RAF St Athan to handle the servicing of most types of current RAF aircraft. In addition, No 30 MU at RAF Sealand is the main airborne electronic and instrument engineering unit, servicing over 100,000 items per year, not only for the RAF but also the Army, RN and MoD research stations.

The Field Repair Squadron at RAF Abingdon has teams of tradesmen who are sent to operational stations where they undertake modification and repairs to aircraft which are beyond the capabilities of unit personnel but do not require returning to an MU. In addition, techniques are developed for battle damage repairs. The Unit is also responsible for salvaging crashed aircraft for all three services plus transporting and erecting aircraft for recruiting displays and exhibitions throughout the country.

In maintaining signals, RAF Support

The Chipmunk T.10 has been the RAF's basic training aircraft since the service took delivery of the first of 635 aircraft in 1949. From 1976, deliveries of 130 Bulldog T.1s commenced and the Chipmunk strength has been dramatically reduced. The main users are now the Air Cadets and the Flying Selection Squadron. Visible here are Chipmunk T.10s from No 6 AEF and Bulldogs from London UAS and Oxford UAS all of which are based at RAF Abingdon.

Command's responsibilities include the large number of high frequency (HF) facilities used not only by Strike Command but also the Military Air Traffic Organisation, NATO and the Meteorological Office. On the ground, there are the message relay centres, general purpose telephones and air movements networks plus the Skynet Satellite communications system. RAF North Luffenham houses the deep servicing of ground radar and radar equipment whilst RAF Digby provides training for men in the mast construction role.

The three equipment supply depots at RAF Carlisle, RAF Quedgeley and RAF Stafford hold and supply about a million different types of technical and domestic equipment on behalf of RAF Support Command for RAF use together with air stores and accommodation stores for the Army and RN. Through a computer system installed at RAF Hendon and linked to about 100 stations, urgent demands can be processed within six hours and low priority requirements satisfied within seven days. This has resulted in great savings in the size of stock holding as well as giving faster turn rounds on requests for any item.

Finally, RAF Support Command provides administration support not only for the functional units within the Command but also for some 140 units in the UK and overseas. In October 1985, a fire at RAF Brampton destroyed the Headquarters building but, due to the efficiency of the administration, it was fully functioning within four days from hastily erected temporary buildings. A major part of this support is devoted to the medical services, and it controls hospitals at RAF Ely, RAF Halton and RAF Wroughton plus the rehabilitation units at Chessington and Headley Court.

In all, RAF Support Command embraces over 200 units and has a total strength of about 48,000 personnel, including 12,500 civilians, and nearly 500 aircraft. Amongst the units are five flying training schools, three technical training schools, seven maintenance units, three hospitals, sixteen university air squadrons, thirteen air experience flights, twenty-seven gliding schools, seventy-one career information offices and thirteen US bases.

Support Command

Unit	Aircraft	Location
No 1 Flying Training School	Jet Provost T.5	Linton on Ouse
No 2 Flying Training School	Gazelle HT.3; Wessex HC.2	Shawbury
No 4 Flying Training School	Hawk T.1	Valley
No 6 Flying Training School	Jet Provost T.5; Dominie T.1; Jetstream T.1	Finningley
No 7 Flying Training School	Jet Provost T.3A, T.5A	Church Fenton
RAF College	Jet Provost T.5A	Cranwell
Central Air Traffic Control School	Jet Provost T.4	Shawbury
Flying Selection Sqn	Chipmunk T.10	Swinderby
Central Flying School	Gazelle HT.3	Shawbury
	Hawk T.1	Valley
	Jet Provost T.5	Scampton
Institute of Aviation Medicine	Hunter T.7	Farnborough
No 1 School of Tech. Training	—	Halton
No 2 School of Tech. Training	—	Cosford
No 4 School of Tech. Training	—	St Athan
No 1 Aircraft Maintenance Sqn	—	Abingdon
No 2 Aircraft Maintenance Sqn	—	Abingdon
No 7 Maintenance Unit	—	Quedgeley
No 11 Maintenance Unit	—	Chilmark
No 14 Maintenance Unit	—	Carlisle
No 16 Maintenance Unit	—	Stafford
No 30 Maintenance Unit	—	Sealand
No 217 Maintenance Unit	—	Cardington

FSS *Above*

All the prospective pilots who have not logged 30 hours' of recognised flying training prior to entry to the RAF are required to take a fifteen-hour flying course at the Flying Selection School (FSS) based at RAF Swinderbury. Here, they are assessed for their suitability for further training in the Jet Provost before joining one of the FTS.

No 1 FTS *Left*

No 1 Flying Training School (FTS), based at RAF Linton-on-Ouse, is equipped with the Jet Provost T.3A and T.5A. Together with No 7 FTS, it accepts student pilots from the FSS for the basic course during which the students will accumulate approximately 60 hours on the Jet Provost T.3A. At this point, successful students will be streamed either for fast jet, in which case they will fly another 55 hours on the Jet Provost T.5A, or for multi-engine or helicopters, flying in both cases an additional 30-odd hours on the Jet Provost T.3A.

The Jet Provost, which was directly developed from the piston-engined Percival Provost, is an extremely docile aircraft but can give a lively aerobatic performance. Thus the aeroplane is an ideal trainer and can be used from the ab initio stage to the point where the student is proficient and confident for the next stage—for those on fast jet, this will be the Hawk T.1 at No 4 FTS.

No 2 FTS, No 1 Squadron

Based at RAF Shawbury, No 2 FTS is split into two squadrons. No 1 Squadron, flying the Gazelle HT.3, and No 2 Squadron, flying the Wessex HC.2. Both the Gazelle and Wessex are used to give student pilots streamed from Nos 1 and 7 FTS their helicopter training. The Gazelles at RAF Shawbury are shared with those of the CFS detachment. The students commence their 28-week course by flying the Gazelle HT.3 for approximately 80 hours, during which they will learn to master basic helicopter flying techniques before progressing on to the Wessex.

No 2 FTS, No 2 Squadron

After completing the Gazelle course, student pilots progress to No 2 Squadron and the Wessex HC.2 on which they will fly a further 50 hours, learning the techniques of flying a larger helicopter and putting their earlier training into context. This will include learning to fly in enclosed spaces and carrying underslung loads.

No 4 FTS

The role of No 4 FTS is to train student pilots who have been selected for fast jet training. No 4 FTS had been equipped with Hunters and Gnats but from 1976 these started to be replaced by some of the 176 Hawk T.1s ordered for the RAF. The Hawk is a highly advanced jet trainer, stressed to +8 and −4 g, and is able to give the student pilots the necessary fast, low level experience as well as fast jet general handling experience without using up the valuable expensive airframe hours of operational aircraft when he gets to the OCU.

No 6 FTS

No 6 FTS, based at RAF Finningley, conducts a wide range of crew training, a variety of types being operated. Navigators undertake a 29-week training course, of which 44 hours are flown at high level, using the Dominie T.1. At this point, the student probably knows where his first posting is likely to be and he commences a further 20 hours in the Jet Provost T.5 undertaking the type of flying which he is likely to encounter during his operational flying. The Dominie T.1 is also used for training the air electronic operators (AEO).

Left: The Dominie T.1 is a military training version of the HS.125. Twenty entered RAF service in the mid 1960s. Two stations are provided for the students plus a position for the instructor and another for a supernumerary. The student's position contains a variety of equipment, including HF, VHF and UHF radio, Decca navigator, gyro-magnetic compass, ILS, ADF, weather radar, Doppler, ground-position indicator and VHF Omni-Range (VDR).

Right: Top to bottom, Dominie, Jetstream and Jet Provost. No 6 FTS uses the Jetstream T.1 for training multi-engined pilots and to a lesser degree Air Engineers, AEO's and navigators.

Central Flying School

The CFS operates the Jet Provost T.3A and T.5 variants for basic jet training of the student instructors. The Hunting Jet Provost T.1 was a conversion of the piston-engined Provost T.1 to the jet power of the Bristol Siddeley Viper and became the standard basic trainer for the RAF. The Jet Provost T.3 was the improved version of the Jet Provost T.1.

CFS

Over the years, the CFS has supplied the RAF with many of its aerobatic teams on most of the types of aircraft it has operated. Illustrated are Jet Provost T.5s painted in the markings of the Red Pelicans.

The CFS Hawk T.1

Apart from the Red Arrows based at RAF Scampton the CFS uses the Hawk T.1 to train instructors. These are based alongside those of No 4 FTS at RAF Valley.

Red Arrows

In addition to the Hawks operated by the CFS detachment based at RAF Valley the world famous Red Arrows who also fly the Hawk are part of the CFS and are based at RAF Scamp- ton. The Red Arrows can be seen over the Niagara Falls during a tour of North America.

CFS

In July 1975, the CFS became the first RAF unit to receive the Scottish Aviation Bulldog T.1 as a replacement for its Chipmunks. Powered by a 200 hp Avco-Lycoming the Bulldog is capable of 185 knots and is fully aerobatic. It also serves with the Swedish, Nigerian and Malaysian Armed Forces.

RAFC

The Royal Air Force College at Cranwell undertakes the Initial Officer Training. Following this members of the University Air Squadrons (UAS) remain at the RAFC together with those who have the necessary flying experience such as having gained their own PPLs; the balance join the FSS. Those who have stayed at RAFC will spend 31 weeks flying the Jet Provost T.5A before streaming. Those selected for fast jets continue their instruction before moving on to the Hawk while the others move straight on to their next training school. The picturesque RAF College buildings can be in the background of this Jet Provost T.5 overflying the airfield.

UAS

There are 16 University Air Squadrons located around the UK and providing facilities for university undergraduates to experience RAF life and gain some flying tuition. These may consist of students who have been sponsored by the RAF and are committed to joining the Service, but may also include students who are interested in the RAF but are not so positive as to their future plans. All of this flying is carried out on the Bulldog T.1 of which a total of 130 was ordered for RAF use. The Bulldog is the military version of the Pup, originally designed by Beagle but with a larger strengthened wing. A basic side-by-side fully aerobatic trainer, which was built by Scottish Aviation, it has almost completely replaced the Chipmunk.

Air Cadets

The Air Cadets have one facility that no other national youth organisation has—the opportunity to learn to fly. Through the Air Training Corps (ATC) or the RAF branch of the Combined Cadet Force (CCF), eligible cadets can have a 25 minute flight in a Chipmunk, Bulldog or Husky at one of the thirteen air experience flights throughout the UK. In addition, 27 volunteer gliding schools (VGS), spread throughout the UK, have the primary function of providing proficiency training to solo standard; a total of some 1,500 air cadets pass annually.

The VGS have an important task, familiarisation gliding for the younger cadets. RAF Syerston houses the Central Gliding School (CGS) where new instructors are trained. The Kirby Cadet Mk 3 and the Sedberg have provided the backbone of Air Cadet gliders since the 1950s. These are now gradually being replaced by several new types. Venture self-launching gliders were the first to be introduced, a total of 40 from 1977. In 1983, five ASW 19 high-performance gliders were accepted and named Valiant, together with two Janus C to replace the Swallows and ten ASK 21 tandem-seat gliders named Vanguard. In 1984, the first of 100 Grob Acros was delivered. Named Viking, it is eventually to replace the Cadet Mk 3 and the Sedberg which had been withdrawn by the end of 1986.

The total cost of the re-equipment was about £2 m. Whilst not an inconsiderable sum, it will prove good value encouraging more youngsters to join the Air Cadets and eventually the Services well into the next century.

Air Cadets—Newton

Central Gliding School	Viking TX.1; Valiant TX.1; Janus; Vanguard TX.1; Venture T.2; Grasshopper TX.1	Syerston
No 13 AEF	Bulldog T.1	Belfast
No 618 VGS	Valiant TX.1; Vanguard TX.1	West Malling
Nos 623 and 642 VGS	Not yet allocated	Not yet allocated

Chipmunk T.10 equipped AEFs

No 1 AEF—Manston	No 2 AEF—Hurn	No 3 AEF—Filton
No 4 AEF—Exeter	No 5 AEF—Cambridge	No 6 AEF—Abingdon
No 7 AEF—Newton	No 8 AEF—Cosford	No 9 AEF—Finningley
No 10 AEF—Woodvale	No 11AEF—Leeming	No 12 AEF—Turnhouse

Venture T.2 equipped VGS

No 611 VGS—Swanton Morley	No 612 VGS—Benson	No 613 VGS—Halton
No 616 VGS—Henlow	No 624 VGS—Chivenor	No 632 VGS—Ternhill
No 633 VGS—Cosford	No 635 VGS—Salmesbury	No 637 VGS—L Rissington
No 642 VGS—Linton on Ouse	No 644 VGS—Syerston	No 664 VGS—Bishops Court

Viking TX.1 equipped VGS

No 614 VGS—Wethersfield	No 615 VGS—Kenley	No 617 VGS—Manston
No 622 VGS—Upavon	No 625 VGS—South Cerney	No 626 VGS—Predannon
No 631 VGS—Sealand	No 634 VGS—St Athan	No 636 VGS—Swansea
No 643 VGS—Scampton	No 645 VGS—Catterick	No 661 VGS—Kirknewton
No 662 VGS—Arbroath	No 663 VGS—Kinloss	

University Air Squadrons—Cranwell

Aberdeen, Dundee and St Andrews — Leuchars	East Midlands — Newton	Oxford — Abingdon
Birmingham — Cosford	Glasgow and Strathclyde — Glasgow	Queen's — Belfast
Bristol — Filton	Liverpool — Woodvale	Southampton — Hurn
Cambridge — Cambridge	London — Abingdon	Wales — St Athan
East Lowlands — Turnhouse	Manchester and Salford — Woodvale	Yorkshire — Finningley
	Northumbrian — Leeming	

No 5 AEF at Cambridge is unique in having a Beagle Husky on its strength. The aircraft was won in a raffle in aid of the National Society for Mentally Handicapped Children by Mr Fred Pontin. He gave it back to the Society who asked Mr Hughie Green to find an organisation who could use it usefully. Mr Billy Butlin bought it and generously presented it to the Air Training Corps on 16 January 1969. By 1986, it had completed some 5,000 hours of air experience flying with No 5 AEF.

The Chipmunk T.10 is the standard equipment of the AEFs although No 13 AEF at Sydenham operates a Bulldog T.1 which enables it to share the servicing of Queen's UAS.

The AEFs were formed in 1958, equipped with 50 Chipmunks. There are now 51 Chipmunks allocated to twelve AEFs. They give cadets a chance to fly and even to take the controls. The Chipmunk T.10 was designed by de Havilland Canada as a tandem-seat basic trainer. It has seen sterling service within the RAF. Although largely withdrawn from RAF service, those flying with the AEFs will continue their role for some years to come. Chipmunks from No 5 AEF based at Cambridge Airport are illustrated.

A few of the 95 Grasshoppers remain, mainly with Combined Cadet Force units for whom they give a very basic practical experience of the principles of flying.

The Kirby Cadet Mk 3 has seen sterling service since the early 1950s with the Air Cadets. It has been numerically the largest type, with 124 having been ordered from Slingsby. Built from a wooden structure and covered in fabric, it has proved to be a very robust glider. By the end of 1986, they should have been replaced by the Viking TX.1. This particular Cadet Mk 3 is from No 617 VGS and can be seen over its home base at RAF Manston.

In addition to the Cadet Mk 3, the VGS of the Air Cadets have also operated 93 Sedbergs, in a mixed fleet. With the Sedberg having side-by-side seating, it has been used mainly for air experience gliding whilst the Cadet Mk 3 was used for proficiency training. These will also be replaced by the Viking TX.1 by the end of 1986. This Sedberg is from No 617 VGS at RAF Manston.

Slingsby built 40 SF-25C Falke self-launching gliders for the Air Cadets. It is powered by a 1600 cc Rollason-Volkswagen engine and requires only a minimum of ground crew and equipment. The longer flight duration enables more efficient concentrated instruction. This Venture T.2 is from No 612 VGS based at RAF Benson.

The Grob G.103 Twin II Acro, known as Viking TX.1 in Air Cadets service, is rapidly becoming the backbone of the VGS as deliveries of the 100 gliders arrive to replace the Cadet Mk 3 and the Sedberg. These gliders are of glass fibre construction which is not only more easily repaired than the Cadet and Sedberg but with its qualities allow the use of modern aerodynamics, giving a far superior performance. In addition, they are fitted with a 720-channel radio, enabling easy communications, and a cockpit canopy which provides a degree of comfort not experienced before in Air Cadet gliding. No 622 VGS at RAF Upavon was the third unit to receive the Viking.

The Valiant TX.1 is the Air Cadets' version of the Schleicher ASW 19, of which five were ordered to replace the Swallows at CGS for training instructors. This Valiant TX.1 belongs to No 618 VGS at West Malling where it is used in the additional role of cadet advanced training.

CATCS

The Central Air Traffic Control School (CATCS) at RAF Shawbury flies a number of Jet Provost T.4s. These are used to give the trainee Air Traffic Controllers practical experience of handling real aircraft as well as giving them flights in the aircraft so that they can experience some of the problems that the pilot encounters from his end.

The Vanguard TX.1 is the Air Cadets' version of the Schleicher ASK 21, of which ten were ordered and delivered during 1983. The Vanguard is visually very similar to the Viking. At the naming ceremony, it was felt that these would become the standard glider for the Air Cadets but it proved not to be so, and the type only equips No 618 VGS at West Malling airfield which is visible in the background.

SOTT

A large number of time expired air-craft are used by the SoTTs to give as much practical experience to the students as possible. Illustrated here is a Jet Provost which has been the subject of some paint spraying instruction and has also had some of its skin removed to assist in teaching the students about the various parts of the aircraft.

Maintenance Units

Major servicing of RAF aircraft is mainly carried out at the maintenance units at RAF Abingdon and RAF St Athan. At the MUs, aircraft are completely stripped down for the required checks to be made and components replaced. Some major servicing is conducted by outside civilian contractors. Here a Jaguar GR.1 is undergoing a major service at RAF Abingdon following its return from service with RAFG. This and the other RAFG Jaguars are then being placed in the storage facility at RAF Shawbury where these and other types are kept pending their issue to the flying units as required.

BBMF

The Battle of Britain Memorial Flight (BBMF) was formed at RAF Biggin Hill in 1957 as a memorial to those who died in the Battle of Britain. The BBMF consists of two Hurricanes, five Spitfires, a Lancaster and a Chipmunk. Each year the BBMF fly the aircraft to many air displays throughout the UK plus a few on the continent. The Chipmunk is used for pilot familiarisation on tail draggers so as to conserve hours on the older aircraft.

The Vintage Pair

The Vintage Pair was made up of a Meteor T.7 and Vampire T.11, representing the RAF's first jet training aircraft. Operated by volunteer ground and aircrews from their base at RAF Scampton, the Vintage Pair were seen at some 50 displays throughout the UK each year.

Sadly, the aircraft were destroyed during a display at Mildenhall in 1986 and two members of the team killed.

RAF Regiment

The RAF Regiment is the Royal Air Force's 'army', and is responsible for the defence of airfields and other installations against ground forces and low-level aircraft attacks. To enable the RAF Regiment to fulfil its commitments, it has split its squadrons into two different roles. Those designated to counter enemy ground forces are equipped with Scorpion light tanks and Spartan armoured personnel carriers plus a Sultan mobile command vehicle and a Samson mobile repair

RAF Regiment—Catterick

No 3 Wing, Strike Command	Nos 51 and 58 Sqns	Light Armour
No 4 Wing, RAF Germany	Nos 16, 26, 37 and 63 Sqns	Rapier
No 5 Wing, Strike Command	Nos 2 and 15 Sqns	Light Armour
No 6 Wing, Strike Command	Nos 19, 20 and 66 Sqns★	Rapier
No 33 Wing, RAF Germany	No 1 Sqn	Light Armour
Strike Command	Nos 27 and 48 Sqns	Rapier
Strike Command	No 34 Sqn	Light Armour
	Queen's Colour Sqn	Field Squadron

★ Based at Brize Norton, Honington and West Raynham respectively and responsible for the defence of some USAFE bases.

Royal Auxiliary Air Force Regiment

No 2503 (County of Lincoln) Sqn — Scampton
No 2620 (County of Norfolk) Sqn — Marham
No 2622 (Highland) Sqn — Lossiemouth
No 2623 (East Anglian) Sqn — Honington
No 2624 (County of Oxford) Sqn — Brize Norton
No 2625 (County of Cornwall) Sqn — St Mawgan
No 2729 (City of Lincoln) Sqn — Waddington

The Rapier is capable of engaging aircraft flying very low at any speed. The missile can be guided by an optical sight or radar and is so accurate that the target is destroyed by a direct rather than a proximity hit. The Rapier crews frequently train in providing a protective ring around their base airfield and on some of these exercises, this can include the simulation of an enemy attack, which requires NBC clothing to be worn. In 1983, No 6 Wing was formed with finance from the USAF. In an emergency, it would use its three squadrons to protect USAF bases in the UK.

vehicle. Those defending against intruding air-craft have given up their Bofors guns and Tigercat missiles for the Rapier surface-to-air missile.

Royal Auxiliary Air Force

In 1979, three Royal Auxiliary Air Force Regiment squadrons were formed, one each at RAF Lossiemouth, Scampton and Honington, which are manned by civilians from the local community. Following action in the South Atlantic in which the Rapier proved to be highly successful, an additional RAuxAF Regiment squadron was formed at RAF Waddington with ex-Argentinian Oerlikon anti-aircraft guns brought back from the Falklands.

RAE

The Royal Aircraft Establishment based at Farnborough has numerous types of aircraft on its strength for a variety of trials in support of aircraft of today and tomorrow. They are painted in a high visibility colour scheme and range in types frm a Dakota to a Tornado. The aircraft are crewed by RAF personnel.

A&AEE

The cessation of conflict in the South Atlantic saw the revival of a function of the Aeroplane and Armament Experimental Establishment (A&AEE) which had not exercised since World War Two: testing enemy aircraft. A number of Pucara ground attack aircraft were brought back to the UK. Most were badly damaged following SAS attacks but one was returned to an airworthy condition. Although the Pucara is built with 1950s technology, it was test flown for 25 hours before being presented to the RAF Museum. Like the Royal Aircraft Establishment Farnborough, A&AEE aircraft are crewed by RAF personnel, although at Farnborough the civilian scientists usually fly with their trials.

Empire Test Pilots School

The main duty of the ETPS based at A&AEE Boscombe Down, involves training operational pilots for test flying duties for the three British Services as well as for other countries. Each year, 22 students, of whom some 50 per cent are from overseas, join the course. The course is designed to help them to understand aircraft from the designer point of view. It also trains them to assess the extremities of the aircraft's flight boundary and accurately to communicate their findings. The ETPS has a variety of aircraft on its strength ranging in performance from the Gazelle to the Lightning. A Beagle Basset has been modified to simulate stability and control characteristics via an analogue computer, modifying the handling inputs and responses. A Hawk has also been modified by the College of Aeronautics at Cranfield to give it variable stability performance for the ETPS. Here, a Lightning T.5 taxies in after a training sortie.

Index

A

A&AEE 125, 126
Air Experience Flights 100, 101, 112, 113, 114
Air Traffic Control 101, 119
Airfields: Abingdon 101, 102, 112, 120;
    Akrotiri 8, 11, 12, 18, 35, 48, 50, 64, 86, 87;
    Aldergrove 13, 40; Arbroath 112; Ascension
    8, 14, 35, 47; Barkston Heath 51; Bawdsey
    51; Belfast 34, 122; Belize City 86; Benson
    13, 14, 41, 112, 116; Bentley Priory 8; Biggin
    Hill 100, 121; Binbrook 51, 52, 53, 54, 55;
    Bishops Court 112; Boscombe Down 126;
    Boulmer 71; Brawdy 51, 52, 68, 70, 71, 83;
    Brize Norton 13, 14, 31, 32, 87, 123;
    Bruggen 24, 88, 89, 90, 95, 96; Cambridge
    112; Catterick 14, 112; Chivenor 51, 67, 69,
    71, 112; Church Fenton 101, 102; Coltishall
    13, 18, 45, 71; Coningsby 51, 52, 62; Cosford
    102, 112; Cranwell 100, 101, 102, 110, 112;
    Cottesmore 14, 28; Culdrose 72, 82; Exeter
    112; Farnborough 46, 102; Filton 112;
    Finningley 71, 83, 101, 102, 106, 112; Gatow
    88, 90, 99; Gibraltar 8, 12; Glasgow 112;
    Gutersloh 88, 90, 91, 92, 96, 98; Halton 102,
    112; Hendon 46, 102; Henlow 101, 112;
    Hong Kong 8; Honington 13, 14, 26, 29, 123,
    124; Hullavington 14; Hurn 112; Kemble
    101; Kenley 112; Kinloss 71, 74, 112;
    Kirknewton 112; Laarbruch 88, 89, 90, 91,
    94; Leconfield 71; Leeming 112; Leuchars
    11, 14, 51, 52, 62, 71, 112; Linton on Ouse
    101, 102, 103, 112; Little Rissington 112;
    Lossiemouth 14, 20, 51, 52, 57, 71, 72, 73,
    123, 124; Lyneham 13; Manston 14, 71, 112,
    115, 116; Marham 13, 14, 25, 26, 123;
    Mildenhall 122; Mount Pleasant 12, 14, 17,
    51, 59, 86; Naval Point 84; Newton 100, 112;
    North Coates 51; North Luffenham 102;
    Northolt 13, 42; Odiham 13, 14, 36; Offutt
    AFB 12; Predannack 112; St Athan 101, 102,
    112, 120; St Mawgan 71, 74; Salmesbury
    112; Scampton 101, 102, 109, 112, 122, 123,
    124; Sealand 101, 102, 112; Sek Kong 12;
    Shawbury 89; South Cerney 112; Stanley 12,
    17, 33, 34, 47, 59, 82, 84; Swansea 112;
    Swanton Morley 112; Swinderbury 120,
    103; Sydenham 113; Syerston 112; Ternhill
    112; Turnhouse 112; Upavon 8, 112, 117;
    Valley 62, 71, 72, 101, 102, 108, 109;
    Waddington 53, 57, 62, 123; Wattisham 51,
    61, 62; West Malling 112, 117, 119; West
    Raynham 51; Wethersfield 112; Wildenrath
    88, 90, 97, 98; Wittering 5, 13, 14, 18;
    Woodvale 112; Wroughton 14; Wyton 51,
    71, 72, 78, 84, 85; Yeovilton 79, 81
ALARM 93
Andover 43, 88; C.1 41, 47, 90, 98; CC.2 13,
    14, 42, 43, 44; E.3 13, 41
APC 11, 12, 64
AV-8B 9

B

Basset 126
BAe 146 13, 32, 43, 44; CC.2 14, 43
BL75S 18
Bloodhound 12, 51; Mk 2 64
Bofor 124
Buccaneer 8, 13, 66, 71, 73, 88, 92, 94, 96; S.2A
    71, 73; S.2B 71, 72
Bulldog 100, 101, 112; T.1 101, 110, 111, 112,
    113

C

C-130E 33; C-130K 33
Cadet Mk 3 112, 115, 116, 117
Canberra 8, 11, 12, 13, 45; B.2 71, 78; T.4 71,
    79; PR.7 71, 78; PR.9 13, 71, 79, 85; E.15 71,
    78; TT.18 71, 78; T.17 71, 79
Chinook 10, 12, 21, 22, 36, 83, 84, 88, 98; HC.1
    13, 14, 39, 86, 90, 96
Chipmunk 100, 112; T.10, 52, 88, 90, 99, 101,
    102, 113, 114, 121
College of Aeronautics 126
Comet 4C 74, 77
Commands: Air Support 11; Bomber 11;
    Coastal 11; Fighter 11; RAFG 18, 24, 64, 73,
    88, 89, 90, 91, 95, 96, 97, 120; Signals 11;
    Strike 8, 11, 45, 87; Support 8, 11, 100, 101,
    102; Training 100

D

DHC Devon 8
Dominie 101; T.1 102, 106

E

E-3A Sentry 12, 53, 55
EAP 52
ECM 24, 71, 73, 79
EFA 52
ELINT 71, 74, 84
ESM 74, 77
Ethiopia 34, 35

F

F-5E Tiger 11, 53
F-11iK 72
Falklands 10, 12, 17, 34, 35, 47, 75, 82, 84, 88,
    121
Flights: No 1310 12, 84; No 1312 12, 14, 33,
    47, 59, 86; No 1417 14, 17, 39, 86; No 1453
    12, 17; No 1563 14, 39, 86; No 1564 12, 82,
    84; Andover Training Flight 14; Battle
    Flight 97; Battle of Britain Memorial Flight
    2, 52; Berlin Station Flight 88, 90, 91;
    Lightning Augmentation Flight 52, 55;
    Lightning Training Flight 51, 52, 56; Sea
    King Training Flight 72, 82; Search and
    Rescue Training Flight 72, 81; The Queen's
    Flight 13, 14, 32, 42, 43, 44

G

Gannet 53, 57
Gazelle 101, 126; HT.3 89, 102, 104; HCC.4
    13, 42
Gnat 106
Grasshopper 114
Groups: No 1 8, 11, 13; No 11 8, 11, 30, 51, 53;
    No 18 8, 11, 71, 73; No 90 11

H

Harpoon 75
Harrier 33, 39, 88, 89, 95, 96; GR.1 14; T.2 14;
    GR.3 5, 9, 12, 13, 14, 17, 86, 90, 91, 92, 98;
    T.4 5, 13, 14, 17, 90, 92; GR.5 9, 10, 13
Hawk 12, 51, 68, 70, 101, 109, 110, 126; T.1 51,
    52, 66, 67, 69, 102, 103, 106, 108; T.1A 51,
    52, 67
Hercules 13, 14, 33, 34, 47; C.1 14, 33, 34, 36;
    C.1K 12, 14, 33, 35, 47, 59, 86; C.1P 14, 33,
    34, 47; C.3 14, 33
HS 125 8, 42, 106; CC.1 13; CC.2 13; CC.3 13
Hunter 8, 67, 106; T.7 71, 102
Hurricane 121; Mk IIC 52

I

Initial Officer Training 100, 101

J

Jaguar 8, 13, 68, 88, 89, 91, 95; GR.1 13, 14,
    18, 20, 45, 90, 93, 96, 120; T.2 13, 14, 20, 90
Janus C 112
Jet Provost 10, 101, 102, 120; T.3A 102, 103;
    T.4 51, 52, 67, 102, 119; T.5 102, 106, 108;
    T.5A 102, 103, 110
Jetstream 101; T.1 102, 106
JP233 29, 92

K

KC-10 50

L

Lancaster 121; B.I 52
Lightning 8, 11, 12, 51, 52, 53, 54, 55, 56, 126;
    F.3 51, 52, 54; T.5 51, 52, 54, 56, 126; F.6
    51, 52, 53, 54
Lincoln 8
Locations: Aldershot 101; Belize 14, 17, 39;
    Berlin 88, 99; Bracknell 100; Brampton 8,
    100, 102; Cardington 102; Carlisle 102;
    Chessington 102; Chilmark 102; Fylindales
    53; Goose Bay 12; Headley Court 102;
    Hendon 46, 102; High Wycombe 8, 11;
    Mexico City 39; Mount Batten 72; Mount
    Wise 71; Northwood 8, 72; Pitreavie Castle
    71, 72; Quedgeley 102; Rheindahlen 88, 90;
    Stafford 102; Uxbridge 87; Wroughton 102
LRMTS 17, 18

M

Martel 72, 73
MATO 87, 102
Medivac 31
Meteor T.7 122
Meteorological Office 102

N

NATO 11, 12, 13, 24, 53, 62, 79, 88, 90, 97, 102
Nimrod 47, 53, 57, 71, 74, 77; MR.2 71;
    MR.2P 75; AEW.3 12, 53, 57, 75; R.1 71, 84

O

Oerlikon 124
Offshore Tapestry 75
Operations: BUSHELL 34; CORPORATE 34, 47

P

Pembroke 88, 90, 98
Phantom 8, 10, 11, 12, 17, 33, 51, 59, 61, 62;
    FG.1 51, 61, 64; FGR.2 12, 52, 59, 61, 86,
    88, 90, 97; F.3 51, 62
Provost 103
Pucara 125
Puma 13, 88; HC.1 13, 14, 21, 33, 39, 86, 90,
    96, 98

R

RAE 46, 124
Rapier 12, 52, 86, 89, 90, 123, 124
RAF Regiment 12, 13, 123
    Sqns: No 1 89, 90, 123; No 2 14, 123; No 15
    14, 123; No 16 90, 123; No 19 123; No 20
    123; No 26 90, 123; No 27 52, 123; No 34 86,

123; No 37 90, 123; No 48 52, 123; No 51 14, 123; No 58 14, 123; No 60 123; No 63 90, 123; Queen's Colour Sqn 123
Wings: No 3 123; No 4 90, 123; No 5 123; No 6 123; No 33 89, 90, 123
Red Pelicans 108
Red Top 53, 54
Royal Auxiliary AF 10
Sqns: No 1 (County of Hertford) 72; No 2 (County of Edinburgh) 72; No 3 (County of Devon) 73; No 4624 14; No 4626 14
Royal Engineers 89, 90
Royal Navy 17, 53, 57, 59, 61, 72, 73, 79, 83, 87, 101, 102

S
Schools: Central Air Traffic Control School 102, 119
Central Flying School 101, 102, 104, 108, 109, 110
Central Gliding School 112, 117
Empire Test Pilot School 126
Fire Fighting School 14
Flying Training Schools: No 1 101, 102, 103, 104; No 2 101, 104; No 4 101, 103, 106, 108; No 6 101, 106; No 7 101, 103, 104
RAF College 100, 101, 102, 110; RAF Staff College 100; Recruit Training School 100
Schools of Technical Training 120; No 1 102; No 2 102; No 4 102
Volunteer Gliding Schools (VGS) 112, 115, 116, 117
Scorpion 89, 123
Sea Eagle 66, 71, 72
Sea King 8, 71; HAR.3 12, 13, 71, 82, 83, 84, 86
Sea Harrier 9, 17, 59, 66
Sedberg 11, 116, 117
SF-25C Falke 116
Shackleton 8, 51, 53, 57; AEW.2 12, 51, 57
Sidewinder 17, 51, 59, 62, 67, 75
Skyflash 59, 64
Skynet 4a 10, 102
Skyshadow 24
Sparrow 64
Spartan 89, 123
Spitfire 2, 121; Mk II 52; Mk Vb 52; PR.19 52
Squadrons, RAF: No 1 13, 14, 18; No 2 90, 91;

No 3 18, 90, 91; No 4 18, 90, 91; No 5 51, 53; No 6 13, 18; No 7 13, 21, 36, 83; No 8 51, 57; No 9 24, 90; No 10 13, 14, 35; No 11 51; No 12 71, 72, 73; No 14 90, 91, 93; No 15 90, 92, 94; No 16 90, 94; No 17 90, 95; No 18 90, 96; No 19 90, 97; No 20 95; No 22 71, 81, 83, 84; No 23 10, 12, 33, 51, 59, 86; No 24 13, 33, 34, 47; No 25 51, 64; No 27 13, 25, 27; No 28 12, 86; No 29 51, 59; No 30 13, 33, 35, 47; No 31 90, 96; No 32 13, 42, 44; No 33 13, 36; No 41 13, 45; No 42 71, 74; No 43 51, 59, 62; No 45 13, 14, 26, 29; No 47 13; No 51 71, 74, 84; No 54 13, 18; No 55 13; No 56 51, 61; No 57 47, 48; No 60 42, 90, 98; No 63 51, 69; No 64 51, 62; No 70 13, 33, 35; No 72 13, 40; No 74 10, 51, 62; No 78 13, 27, 84, 86; No 79 51, 67; No 84 12, 86, 87; No 85 51, 64; No 90 46; No 92 90, 97; No 100 11, 12, 71, 78; No 101 13, 49; No 111 11, 51, 64; No 120 71, 74; No 115 13, 14, 41; No 151 51, 70; No 201 71, 74; No 202 71, 82, 83, 84; No 206 71, 74; No 214 46; No 216 14, 50; No 230 90, 98; No 234 51, 68; No 360 71, 79; No 617 14, 26; No 706 82 102
Aircraft Maintenance Sqns: No 1 102; No 2 102
Field Repair Squadron 101
Flying Selection Squadron 100, 101, 102, 103, 110
RN Elementary Flying Training Sqn 101
No 227 TFTAS 53
Stingray 75
Sultan 123
Swallow 112, 117

T
Tigercat 124
Tornado 8, 66, 73, 88, 89; GR.1 (IDS) 8, 14, 24, 26, 88, 90, 92, 93, 94, 95, 96; GR(T).1 14; F.2 (ADV) 2, 12, 30, 51, 52; F.3 8, 30, 52
Tristar 10, 13, 31, 32, 46, 47, 50; K.1 14; KC.1 14
TSR.2 59, 73
Tucano 7, 10

U
Units: 2 ATAF 88; 2 TAF 88; Air Cadets 100, 101, 112, 115, 116, 117, 119; Air Training Corps 100, 112, 113; Combined Cadet Force

100, 112, 114
FTS: No 2 22, 39, 59; No 4 FTS 62
Institute of Aviation Medicine 102
MUs: No 7 102; No 11 102; No 14 102; No 16 102; No 30 101, 102; No 217 102; No 431 89, 90
No 1(Br) Corps 88, 92, 96, 98
OCUs 101, 106: No 226 14, 20, 56; No 228 51, 52, 62; No 229 2, 30, 51, 52; No 231 71, 79; No 232 47; No 233 5, 14, 18; No 236 71; No 237 71, 73, 74; No 240 13, 22, 39; No 241 14, 32, 44; No 242 OCU 14, 33, 36
Officer & Aircrew Selection Centre 100
TTTE 14, 28; TWCU 13, 14, 26, 29
TWU 12, 51, 62; No 1 51, 52, 67, 69; No 2 51, 52, 68, 70
Wings: Kinloss 71; Lyneham Tactical 13, 14, 33; St Mawgan 71
University Air Squadrons: Aberdeen, Dundee & St Andrews 112; Birmingham UAS 112; Bristol UAS 112; Cambridge UAS 112; East Lowlands UAS 112; East Midlands 112; Glasgow & Strathclyde 112; Liverpool 112; London 101, 112; Manchester & Salford 112; Northumbrian 112; Oxford 101, 112; Queens 112, 113; Southampton 112; Wales 112; Yorkshire 112

V
Valiant 46, 47, 112; TX.1 117
Vampire T.11 122
Vanguard 112; TX.1 119
VC.10 10, 12, 32, 34, 47; C.1 13, 14, 31, 35, 44; K.2 13, 47; K.3 13, 47, 49
Venture 112; T.2 116
Victor 8, 10, 12, 13, 47, 48; K.1 47; K.1a 47; K.2 13, 47, 48
Viking 112, 119; TX.1 115, 116, 117
Vintage Pair 122
Vulcan 7, 8, 13, 45, 47; B.2 24
Vulcan gun 64

W
Wessex 8, 13, 44, 71, 82, 83, 101; HC.2 13, 40, 71, 81, 86, 102, 104; HCC.4 14, 42; HU.5 86, 87
Whirlwind 8, 71, 81, 87